Embalming Mom

sightline books

The Iowa Series in Literary Nonfiction

Patricia Hampl & Carl H. Klaus, series editors

Janet Burroway
Embalming
Mom
Essays in Life

University of Iowa Press ψ Iowa City

University of Iowa Press, Iowa City 52242
Copyright © 2002 by Janet Burroway
Printed in the United States of America
Design by Richard Hendel
http://www.uiowa.edu/~uipress

The publication of this book was generously
supported by the University of Iowa Foundation.

Printed on acid-free paper

Library of Congress
Cataloging-in-Publication Data

Burroway, Janet.
   Embalming mom: essays in life / by Janet Burroway.
      p.   cm.—(Sightline books: the Iowa series in
   literary nonfiction)
   ISBN 0-87745-790-5 (cloth)
      1. Burroway, Janet.   2. Novelists, American—
   20th century—Biography.   I. Title.   II. Sightline
   books.
   PS3552.U76 Z464   2002
   813'.54—dc21
   [B]   2001046307

02   03   04   05   06   C   5   4   3   2   1

FOR PETER

"One eye filled with blueprints,

One eye filled with light."

Contents

Embalming Mom

I Didn't Know Sylvia Plath

> *. . . because to be Jewish — or Irish or Italian or African-American or, for that matter, a woman of the fifties caught up in the first faint stirrings of feminism — was to be compelled to fake it in a thousand small ways, to pass as one thing when, deep inside, you were something else.*
>
> *— Malcolm Gladwell, "True Colors"*

The note in my Cambridge Pocket Diary for Saturday, May 7, 1960, reads "Ted & Sylvia dinner," but doesn't give an hour or an address. The diary otherwise contains a wonder of information. Two and a half inches by four, its tissue-thin pages massed to a mere quarter-inch, it nevertheless records the hour of every sunrise and -set, dates of eclipses and bank holidays, the schedules of trains, coaches, libraries, botanical gardens, and the closing of the Back Gates. It lists academic society meetings for Lent, Michaelmas, and Easter terms; the rugby, hockey, and cricket meets; the Moveable Feasts; the university officers; and the phone numbers of the colleges — though in my experience no student had a phone. It gives the Order of the Boats. It dates the dread Exams.

My own penciled entries are more tantalizing. Paging backward from the Ted and Sylvia dinner, I easily recall (David) "Daiches" and "Maggie" (Drabble) and "Eleanor" (Bron), but not "Fenner's" or "Braithewaite" or "Jack." There was a "Commemoration Dinner" on Saturday April 23, but what it commemorated I no longer memorate. I remember the meeting with "Dadie" (Rylands), and — here it is: Thursday, April 21, "Faber—6:00."

That was the publisher's reception at Russell Square where we'd run into each other, and about which Sylvia wrote to her mother and brother on April 26, excited to be back among the literati, preening at others' amazement that she had given birth only three weeks before. The tone of her letter is postpartum-manic, the description of the party sandwiched between plans for dinner with the Spenders and the Eliots and news of her success with poems at the *Atlantic Monthly*. She describes me as a "lively American girl" whose novel Faber is publishing and "whose path crossed mine often in America," and mentions that she has invited me and my Indian poet friend to spaghetti dinner. Then she goes on to boast of her husband's arty friends, and of drinking champagne while feeling "very grand and proud of Ted."

The Faber reception took place in the heady spring of the Hugheses' burgeoning: their daughter's birth, a book apiece, projects for the BBC, even the flow of a little money. It would be nearly three years before the marriage blew apart, before Sylvia wrote her great poems and committed suicide, and so set in motion a hagiographic industry. At the time it must have seemed that fame could be grasped as an act of will, with no more *sturm* than ambition had already stirred in them.

But I don't know that. I didn't know Sylvia Plath, and this piece is not about her but about me — or about a particular kind of lit-and-print-mad girl of the fifties, whose thwarted hunger augured a shift in what we mean by marriage.

The paths Sylvia mentions had crossed more often than we ourselves had met. I had followed her at *Seventeen*, *Mademoiselle*, Mount Holyoke's Glascock Poetry Contest, and Cambridge University. As winners in that prize round, precursors partly of liberation but also of the brat pack of the eighties, we had lived in separate years at the Barbizon Hotel in Manhattan and at Whitstead House in Cambridge; had at separate times worked under Cyrilly Abels and Polly Weaver at *Mademoiselle*; studied Tragedy with Kathleen Burton at Cambridge and gone to David Daiches's lectures on the Modern Novel; published in the university magazine *Granta*; suffered through Miss Abbott's stilted teas and Mrs. Milne's Sunday morning kippers at Whitstead House; and been the token leggy American at the Amateur Dramatic Club. Now I had like Ted landed in the Faber stable, to be curried by the portly editor Charles Monteith, who was both kind and shrewd.

But there were oddities in that crossing of roads-less-traveled. The annual *Mademoiselle* Guest Editor Contest brought twenty young women to New York for the month of June to work on the College Issue of the magazine. I had won this jaunt from the University of Arizona in 1955, two years after Sylvia, and my first assignment was to write a news item on her Glascock Prize. I had never heard of Sylvia Plath. I struggled in a sort of remote-controlled envy to arrange the boring facts. I wrote home, "I'm so sick of writing little news stories and having them edited from bad to worse." I was taken off that job and set to writing the College Issue's editorial, the required perky tone of which set my teeth on edge. I complained to my parents, "Couldn't they just *call* us something else? So far we haven't been treated like guests and we certainly haven't edited." The interns that year included Joan Didion and Jane Truslow (who became my one confidante among the group, and would later marry Sylvia's former boyfriend Peter Davison), writer Gael Greene and designer Adrienne Steckling, and fifteen others in various stages of anxiety, ambition, and self-doubt. I was sometimes dismissive of my fellow GEs, sometimes grateful; sometimes "everyone else seemed to know what they were doing and seemed to be getting it done fast and well." My desert background was a dubious badge; I flaunted it, but deep inside I knew I was a yokel. I recoiled from Betsy Talbot Blackwell, who sailed between the mirrors of the editorial room waving her cigarette holder, adjuring us to "Believe in Pink." But I admitted in my letters that, "Personally, I think parts of it have been pretty glamorous." Sylvia's fictional evocation of the *Mademoiselle* month in *The Bell Jar* was eight years away. We were made gifts of, stuffed into, or ushered along to ogle the fashions that were armored even to their names — *stiletto, sheath, cinch.* Underneath each of us wore the bra that conjured Amazons and was later resurrected by Madonna as outerwear, stitched in stiff concentric circles to a point. Alternately bored and dazzled at photos ops and Trigère showings, depressed and anxious to impress, I faked it in Milliken plaids and an energy that verged on shrill; and it did not then occur to me that any of the others could be scared and judgmental in equal parts. Nor, certainly, did it ever cross my mind that Sylvia Plath might have written at length to her brother about the elation, depression, shock, revelations, exhaustion, apathy of that month of "living very hard and newly."

Sylvia's letters do not describe the pivotal perk of the *Mademoiselle* month, the ball on the roof of the St. Regis, but *The Bell Jar* neatly dismisses its starlit glamour, satirizes the Ivy Leaguers in their "All-American bone structures" on loan to squire the novice editors, and mocks her own fake lamé top above its "big, fat cloud of tulle."

But I was eighteen, a virginal Methodist Phoenix freshman who had never had a cigarette or a drink, not yet blasé about bone structure, and the occasion hornswoggled me entirely. My bodice was flame-colored nylon shirred onto a big, fat cloud of the same stuff. My letter home, written in the middle of the night after the ball, details my earrings, the chandeliers, hors d'oeuvres ("the cheapest thing on the menu is $5.25 and the steaks are $12.50"), dessert and demitasse, "with a waiter pouring fresh gravy on the meat or filling the water glass every time I took a bite," and especially the "unpretty intellectual boy who talked fascinating serious politics and Europe and literature all the way through dinner," a poet on his way to Oxford on a Fulbright Scholarship, who escorted me back to the Barbizon by way of "a ride through Cent. Park in a Hansom Cab. This is the New York I had in mind!"

I am grubbing in the attic now, surprised that my hazy memory of these old letters takes such solid form: the accordion file, the shoebox, the folders; some crumbling, some crisp, all trailing cockroach shit. My father bundled this trove, after my mother died in 1973, into a shiny fifty-gallon garbage can and shipped it by Greyhound bus to me in Tallahassee. The letters from the *Mademoiselle* month are filed in order, and oddly retrieved and interleaved are the letters I sent from there to my high school friend Marilyn. I have a thick chronological stack of the missives I sent from Phoenix and later from New York to the "unpretty intellectual" poet — these because the eventual engagement was of so formal a fifties kind that we returned our letters to each other when it was terminated, a bow to privacy that I now betray. My letters from Cambridge are missing, though I oddly have the postcards and the fistful of envelopes from which those letters disappeared. The later notes from Yale are also gone. The married letters from Binghamton, Belgium, and Sussex, the traumatized outcries of imminent divorce from Champaign, Illinois — those are disarranged, a hodgepodge, evidence of the chaos in both my life and my mother's health.

From Phoenix that summer of 1955, when the *Mademoiselle* College Issue came out, I wrote to the poet who was now my boyfriend, deprecating the awful photos of myself in dacron shirtwaist and pillbox hat, adding:

> Another thing in Mlle you forgot to mention and which I'm sure you must have seen is an absolutely fantastically deep good poem by a beautiful Mt. Holyoke [*sic*] graduate named Sylvia Plath who goes to Cambridge on a Fulbright this year. The whole idea just grits my teeth in horror. Please inform by return mail that you are so blinded by my lovliness [*sic*] that you don't even want to look at another woman or I may be forced to accept a ring this summer. Honestly, when I saw it I just got scared to death. Do you suppose after all these years of not resenting anything ever except other peoples' talent I might turn out to be a jealous wife? Oh, I do hate Sylvia Plath.

It will hardly be necessary to point out which parts of this make me cringe. But I know, too, that nothing is easier than superiority to the callow fool you used to be, and I am less interested in the cloying tone than in clues to the paradox that ripped my generation from cervix to esophagus. I had never so far been jealous of anything except talent. The prospect of a new sexual or romantic jealousy made me — what? — threaten to accept the engagement I had been staving off. I was both afraid to lose him to the competition and afraid to commit. I said as much, admitting to "a reaction that I'm at a loss to interpret — a sort of perpetual excited fear; an intense desire to be with you, and a genuine alarm whenever I think of your proposal or the ring."

Ambivalence about marriage, ambivalence about ambition, an unambiguous sense that these are in opposition to each other — these make up the leitmotif, not perhaps of my whole generation but of the most audible segment of it. My boyfriend joked gallantly, however, that the young poet was actually named Plass but had a lisp; and apparently assigned her other defects, to which I coyly responded, "I just concur all over the place about Sylvia. She probably has dirty fingernails."

By August I was back in New York on a Barnard scholarship, chattering home about engagement rings and the social scene. "Went to Fulbright reception at the English Embassy & of all things, met Sylvia

Plath! (tell Mare this) who is just as nice as possible but doesn't worry me." My boyfriend and Sylvia being members of the same Fulbright group, they sailed together, and I flung into the Atlantic void, "I hope you are completely avoiding Sylvia (after all, Who Is Sylvia?)." But I also recorded with some exhilaration, in a letter to my mother two days before my nineteenth birthday, "one of my fantastic dreams last night in which I was armed with a Fulbright scholarship myself, and a ticket on the Elizabeth, and was to meet [him] on board and simply couldn't get my suitcase closed. The thing was positively alive, and finally I just told you to send it on and jumped on a raft in my levis and paddled out to catch the departing boat, only to find that [he] was sitting with Sylvia Plath, but had a friend picked out for me. Lovely dream."

For the next year and a half I was about-to-be-engaged, engaged, dis-engaged, re-engaged, finally a disgraced breacher of promise. The journey is marked by petulant half-steps and turnings back. "I will take the ring at Christmas," I wrote from New York, "But every time you mention it I cry." "The truth is, tho, Momma, that I just don't want to marry him this summer. I haven't got any logical reason . . . as my brother says, 'You don't have to do anything just because it says so in the paper.'" "I'm not ready to get married, I'm not ready, I'm not ready."

My vacillation and velleity I must now see as bad faith. In these letters to Oxford I am an advanced tease. I accept and gush over the ring, put off the wedding, declare my devotion, moil through my doubts, then apologize groveling, heavy on the adverbs. I had an on-going crush on George Plimpton, who was my composition teacher, and whose every clever saying, word of praise, is recorded home, so that my mother pointed out that he occupied more space in my letters than my fiancé. She urged me to "be sure" before I married — but what was that? I had met a poet on a starlight roof, we wandered in the woods together talking poetry, he was going to England, he wanted to marry me. Not only Hollywood but also the lessons of home — which had been so confusing because my mother presented her own marriage as a film romance whereas I could see that it was not — led me to expect the feelings that did not emerge. There was something wrong with me if I did not love; I must do so, I would do so if only I could adjust. So I waited, argued, twisted in my little-ease, and ultimately drew down an awful, earned anger from his family.

The taste of freedom that Rosie the Riveter felt may ultimately have led her daughters to the barricades. But our mothers were too old to have worked in war factories. Aurelia Plath had been a teacher before her marriage, but, she confesses in the introduction to *Letters Home*, she submitted to her husband's wishes and became a full-time house-wife. My mother had wanted to be an actress but had been prevented by parents who used her ill health as an excuse (the operative reason was that actresses were *wicked*), and she settled for teaching "elocu-tion" lessons at two dollars an hour out of our living room. My fiancé's mother had been a nurse and shocked me by stating flatly that she had never wanted children. These women very naturally perpetuated their enforced priorities. Nor did our professional models differ. I wrote home cheerily that Barnard's President "Millicent McIntosh (who owns the titles Dean, Dr., President, & Professor) says '*Please* call me Mrs.' — very sweet, I think; she says it's the title she's proudest of."

So my incapacity to read my own messages was partly the muddle of the time. In a letter I wrote to my boyfriend as early as December 1955, I find the blatant expression of what became a touchstone, and later a cliché, of the women's movement: "I'm surprised that my ulti-matum about 'obey' in the marriage ceremony effected [*sic*] you the way it did. I meant my tone to be very light, though I really do want it left out. My case, as you call it, is not very well thought out or convincing at all. I just don't think any marriage should be a matter of the man's word over the woman's." However, in January I capitulated (to what eloquence I no longer know): "you win . . . your paragraph and ideas about it are almost lovely, where mine were flip and only half sincere."

As a teenager I had two visions of myself: one stout, tweed-wearing, striding along in the woods alone, writing great verse; the other slop-pily pillowed in voluminous skirts in an overstuffed chair, a semicircle of children at my feet eating cookies I had baked while I read to them. I knew these two images were in conflict. What I didn't understand was that the choice might never be made, that my life could unroll, or lurch, or cascade, with the tension between them constant.

At seventeen, Sylvia grumbled in her journal that she supposed she could reconcile herself to marriage and children, but worried that do-mestic life would swallow up her passion to write. By twenty-two this no longer troubled her. In a letter to Olive Higgins Prouty she said she wasn't "destined" for either academe or a career, and had decided to combine the jobs of writer, mother, and housewife. In January 1956, a month before she was to meet Ted Hughes, she wrote her mother in the same vein. Aurelia should not fear that she would go after a career. On the contrary Sylvia was "definitely *meant* to be married."

To say "ambivalence" is not to say that women of the fifties were duped by genes or society into thinking we wanted families when we didn't — an assumption later condescendingly made on our behalf. The desire to write has no moral validity that can't be accorded the desire to "homemake." What is so, is that all the pressure was in the service of domestic desire, and so all of the rebellion, with its attendant muddle and resentment, came out to defend the writing.

I wrote to Oxford that my mother had admonished me, "to the effect that I should leave your field alone. She's afraid I'm going to 'stress the wrong things in marriage.'" If I expected an ally in my scorn for these ideas, soon I was reassuring him, too: "What success I want for myself, no matter how jealously and passionately I want it, will be entirely apart from and parallel to the success I want for you." His mother struck me speechless by asking point blank and pointedly, if I had to choose between marriage and writing, which I would choose. He wondered whether I couldn't take up one of my other interests, acting or fashion design, in order to avoid competition. In letter after letter I poutingly stood my ground: "I can't help thinking how much easier it would be if I didn't want to write too, and feel so stubbornly convinced that eventually I will be able to do so." When my mother expressed rancor toward my schizophrenic sister-in-law, I took up her case as well: "please stop wishing that B. would give up her music. . . . Don't you see it's the same thing as Mrs. A. wishing I'd forget my foolish notion about writing? I *have* to write, and if she doesn't understand why, it's going to make things tough . . . it isn't going to make me stop writing."

In October of 1955 I began taking a course from W. H. Auden at the Poetry Center of the Young Men's Hebrew Association at Ninety-second and Lexington. By February I was ecstatic about the long-vowel exercises and rhyme schemes in Rolfe Humphries' Y workshop. The next September I enrolled with Louise Bogan and was hired there as a part-time secretary. I described the work to my boyfriend:

I started yesterday at the Poetry Center, and it's a fine job indeed. . . . I go Mondays and Wednesdays from 1 to 6, and have charge of all incoming manuscripts for the Poetry Center Publication Award (Harper's publishing), which is a new thing this year. . . . Moore, Auden and Spender are judging. I catalogue and acknowledge manuscripts and return them as they're rejected. . . . Next week I go buy paraphernalia from punch bowl to ice cubes. . . . I make the refreshments, with two assistants, serve them from 6 to 6:30 to the speaker and audience, greet the speaker or poet and introduce him [*sic*] to whoever.

I now see that this paragraph records in miniature the Poetry Center's part (some will no doubt think for ill) in the future of American Letters. A major prize, a reading series, a round of workshop courses — all of these things were then *avant*.

On November 21, Sylvia wrote home from Cambridge in a breathless boast about Ted's book *The Hawk in the Rain*, which she had just typed in a rush to meet the deadline for the Poetry Center competition. She was superbly confident he would win. The poems, she claimed, were better than anything since Yeats and Dylan Thomas.

She and Ted must have squandered air postage on the manuscript, because it was nine days later that I wrote to Oxford: "The deadline for the Poetry Center contest is today, and so this week the manuscripts have been pouring in; I was run off my feet at work. . . . It is possibly the most valuable job I could have found, for it enables me to see great quantities of what is being done, and to make my own judgments. . . . It so appalls me to see the quantities of horrible stuff doggedly turned out, and even more, the quantities of pretty good."

What I mainly remember from reading the slush pile at the Poetry Center is this heavy sense that for every handful of fine poems or risibly bad ones, there were mountains of a mediocre sort — apparently sincere, sometimes clever, sparking off a little light of truth. I did not then know that I would spend my life teaching young people of this scribblative ilk, nor that the muted depression I felt would later earn my daily bread, but I took the discovery personally and very much to heart.

It never quite struck me how many pathetic cases there must be of people who had as deep desires as I have and simply couldn't make it. . . . They write, they bother editors, they make themselves and their families miserable . . . wanting to write badly enough is not a substitute for talent; and if it were possible now, having found you and your art to live for, I might willingly rid myself of my desire to write (which would make things easier all the way around, I'm bound to admit) but . . . my love of words and inability to leave them alone, my desire to make them obey me and my God Damn it Necessity to make people listen is running down my face and splashing on my typewriter keys.

The letters now were taken up with labyrinthine attempts to defend myself against his family's anger. "Oh, I want to be so humble but I don't think I'm all wrong. I only think I'm fighting all alone against something I can't see. . . . I know my faults I do I do but I'm not hiding them look look here they are I'm selfish I'm ambitious I'm critical."

I lay coiled on my bed. The hours were filled with panic and its double, apathy. I could bear neither to bestow my life nor to be guilty of betrayal. It seemed that my future was already so intertwined with his that if I ripped it free I would not know how to do the simplest things. I had discovered Philip Larkin, and I dulled my angst reciting the poems of his slightly sour and yearning solitude.

I continued to be invited to stiff and awkward evenings at his parents' apartment. Because his father was a doctor (and, I supposed, not subject to the usual rules about outdated medicines) there were little glass shelves full of pills behind metal-rimmed mirrors in the two bathrooms. I stole four bottles of sleeping pills and took them back to the dorm. I don't think I meant to die. I think I had a mild bipolar tendency (which would worsen later with trauma, drink, and the burdens of single parenthood), and that I simply lacked experience at living through depression. But at twenty I didn't know that. I was afraid. I continued to write wrangling, fretful letters, trying to express myself better, to explain my doubts, to extract concessions. I continued numbly to go to class and when at the dorm to lie twisting, listless. I studied the pills and steeled myself to taking them, counting the number of necessary swallows, feeling the cramp and the drowsiness at once, slipping into the last dark lethargy.

One afternoon I came along the central walk that splits the Columbia campus, on my way back from a class to Johnson Hall, conscious of the waiting pills. Walking toward me was a swaggerer in a black leather jacket. This was 1956, very early Beat era. Black leather was still rare on campus, and read tough. As I passed the boy-man, he brought his fist out of his pocket and jabbed it sharply forward. I have no idea why; it was unlikely to have been a threatening gesture, or aimed at me at all. But my imagination was all-tentacles-out, alive with death, and in that second I expected to be stabbed in the stomach. I walked calmly on, also imagining myself lying on the sidewalk barking instructions to the passersby: *Quick! Get somebody! Don't let me die!*

My seven novels revolve in some way around that moment. My books kill off women, especially very young women. It troubles me. At the center of every novel is also a woman who decides, after all, to live.

Still I cowered, and continued to type voluminous letters to Oxford. On February 18, 1957, I wrote:

> The winning manuscript (unanimous from Moore Spender & Auden) is by a young man at Cambridge named Ted Hughes, and is called *Hawk in the Rain*. Actually, he may not be young at all; I guess he could be an older student or a teacher. All three top manuscripts in the contest were from England! which is a little wearying when I think of all the American ones I processed. Interesting phenomenon, too. Think it's significant? I've read some of the Hughes collection, and it is very strong, powerful, difficult, profound and often bitter and bloody. I don't like it much, but I recognize it as good stuff.

On the twenty-fourth, a year to the day after Ted and Sylvia had met, the telegram announcing his win arrived in Cambridge, and Sylvia trumpeted to her mother that they had jumped around the apartment "roaring like mad seals." My fiancé reminded me that he had already sent me news of Ted Hughes's marriage to Sylvia Plass/Plath, and I replied, "I've gone through & through the letters & can't find that Plath clipping. Wasn't it around Christmas?"

I finally, ignominiously, ended the engagement that spring and set about becoming what my now-former fiancé's furious brother described as "a flamboyant dynamo hell-bent on proving to everybody that she's just a terribly big deal." I published a poem in the *Atlantic*, read manuscripts for the *Paris Review*, had a play produced at Barnard, signed with an agent, won the Glascock contest and a Marshall Scholarship to Cambridge. Between my junior and senior years I got a summer job as a temp receptionist on the *New Yorker* ("Momma, can you believe it? I'M GOING TO WORK FOR THE NEW YORKER"). I dated frivolously and often, fell in and out of love with a distinctly unavailable man. For a while I saw television writer Dick Levinson, but "I probably won't go out with him again. . . . We fought and will continue to fight about whether I have a right to write. This kind of thing bores me, and if it's impossible to have a nice simple date without getting into an argument about the rights of women . . . !" The next week I was cooking dinner for him at his place. Nevertheless I exulted. I had saved enough from the summer job not to work in my senior year. "I've been writing, writing, writing. The richness of life overwhelms me . . . 'the glass filled up beyond the brim.'" I wasn't aware that Sylvia Plath was back in Massachusetts, teaching at Smith and mourning the energy she squandered on her classes, but I must have met Ted or both of them on one unremembered occasion, because my battered copy of *The Hawk in the Rain* is signed by him on "20 Oct. 57," and the next day I wrote home: "It's so nice not to feel the weight of a job that consumes the careful reading-time. I did hostess at the poetry center last night, though, for Ted Hughes, a young Englishman, and a startlingly good poet who married Sylvia Plath. . . . He looks very much like George [Plimpton]. Not hard to follow my thought processes, is it?"

When I knew I would be going to Cambridge I wrote my parents in manic bravura: "I am no longer uncertain or afraid about my future; my next two years are being given unaccountably to me in just the way I want to spend them. I am confident that I have a real gift in writing, and a real job to make the most of it; and that job gives me great and constant joy."

At the Faber cocktail party I ran through the Plath parts of my saga for Sylvia. She was in postpartum glow. I remember her glee at being a retrospective object of jealousy, and her impulsive invitation to supper. My Indian poet friend was Zulfikar Ghose, who was cooling his heels in Russell Square because I hadn't been told I could bring a guest and was too green at publishing protocol to ask. My own note home in the intervening fortnight is on a typed postcard, and "dinner with Zulfi, Ted and Sylvia Hughes on Sat." is bracketed with a "decidedly unsettled feeling about the future." Zulfi feared the *Observer* would "send [him] to Scotland or something" to cover the cricket match. Leafing through his old letters, I run across a letter from Sylvia, a clean rectangle of Basildon Bond dated May 3, 1960, typed with one strikeover and one erasure in that wavering pica that is as clear a marker of my youth as black-and-white film stock. She repeats the invitation for that Saturday, promises a simple spaghetti supper, and details the directions via Chalk Farm tube station — the route up Regents Park Road past Gloucester Road, to the white-trimmed gray house that squatted at number 3 among the "squalidia" of Chalcot Square. Her sign-off is cordial and conventional, her signature, in lower case, as round and careful as a schoolgirl's.

A word about *squalidia*. It would be impossible to infer from England today the England of the fifties. Swinging London was not so much as a twinkle in anybody's eye, and the culture shock for the daughters of Betty Crocker was of a grimy kind — dour, fusty, crusted with the penury of spirit that a whole country had learned in war. Decor was tendrilled, bisque, and busy. Cambridge restaurant fare was stodgy-pud, and students couldn't afford it anyhow. Indoors was as damp and cold as out. After a desert childhood and three winters of New York steam heat, I found the brute fact of fen weather made for "living very hard and newly." One of my few surviving letters from Cambridge details a bike ride "down Barton road in the rain, past Newnham pond with a dozen fishers standing in the rain, through Fen Coe all aweep with dropping willows, over a footbridge on the River Cam with the swans hiding eyes under wings from the rain, down Downing into Pembrook streets all gutterglutted with the rain, across Christ's pieces dodging the rain and into the Wesley courtyard to wait in the rain. It has been raining."

My room at Whitstead House, a floor below the one that Sylvia had inhabited, had the standard shilling-fed gas fire in the corner, over which I huddled while the eight fingers outside my book steamed and reddened and my thumbs went numb on the page. Every morning I pulled on a cold wet sweater, coat, and gown and cycled to a lecture hall where my breath blurred the paper on which I scribbled notes through gloves and mittens. Twice a day I slogged across the soggy soccer field for two starches and a pork or mutton chop in Newnham dining hall. In those winters I learned that writing is hard, and not necessarily a constant joy. For me no "big, dark, hunky boy" appeared. I spent a lot of time on Clare Bridge staring into the muddy Cam.

At the same time — and I think this shows through the rainsoaked paragraph above — at Cambridge there was general pride in deprivation. It *felt* as if we were careless of scruff and discomfort, concentrating on higher things. At Barnard the social unit had been perforce the couple, since boys and girls (still called that) were not allowed in each other's rooms, and you had to go somewhere, do something in order to be together. At Cambridge the social unit was the group. Groups formed around subject matter, political sympathy, and choice of genre. They formed more literally around morning coffee, afternoon tea, and evening plonk. There was more sex than at Columbia but publicly less pairing off. The talk was incessant, combative, intricate, exploratory, thrilling. Officially, lectures were optional; supervisions were demanding but once a week. Three-quarters of the learning was done peer-pressured face to face.

And the level of my classmates' talent was so breathtaking that it ended by distorting (perhaps permanently) my assessment of British culture. I shared tea and theater with Eleanor Bron, tutorials with Margaret Drabble. Peter Cook was plotting mayhem *Beyond the Fringe* with Alan Bennett, Dudley Moore, and Jonathan Miller. I acted in a production of *Camino Real* in which Corin Redgrave played Lord Byron, Derek Jacobi and Ian McKellen had minor roles, and the formidable Catherine Stimpson brought the house down as Gypsy with "File this crap under *crap*." John Barton directed Clive Swift as Falstaff, while I scrambled to do Doll Tearsheet in an Irish brogue that would pass muster. Sylvia had complained of dowdy Newnham Dons, but now vivacious Elizabeth Zeeman and porcelain-cool Jean Charlton were organizing English. *Granta* was run by an American triumvirate headed by André Schiffrin; I palled around with them and with their Claremate Jonathan Spence, who had not yet given thought to China. Simon Gray was already sniping from the trenches. David Frost was considered by most of that company an unctuous nothing (and still is). When I went home in the late summer of 1960 it was with the message that the British had it and we didn't — the talent, the intellect, the articulation, the education. It was six years before I returned to England, to realize that the whole country was talking about that Cambridge class. I had unknowingly landed in the crème of the century in the arts.

So Ted and Sylvia were famous among the tyros, but they had not been picked out as icons. The little flat Zulfi and I came to in Chalcot Square was not so much squalid as familiar: shabby stuff chosen with a good eye, care, and flare. I remember the stingy lighting and the sense of the ceiling's being too low for this high couple and their energy. I don't remember what we talked about, though I could reconstruct a likely outline: Faber, Frieda, childbirth, the imminent publication of both *The Colossus* and *Lupercal*, my old clerical role at the Poetry Center, Zulfi's new chapbook series of "Universities Poetry" out of Keele. No doubt I saw to it that the topics included the "first novel" and the "unsettled feeling about the future."

What I remember in particular is this. I stood in the doorway of the narrow kitchen talking with Sylvia, who held Frieda in the crook of her left arm while she rattled pots with her right. The logical thing would have been for me to hold the baby. I may have been too nervous of a five-week-old, or she may have feared Frieda would cry in a stranger's arms. In any case, you can't cook a meal one-handed while rocking an infant, and Sylvia was increasingly brittle, taut. Finally she took the baby into the living room and with some emphasis handed her to Ted — I want to say *shoved her at*. Ted was standing, telling Zulfi how he lay awake at night listening to the owls in the aviary of the London Zoo. He accepted Frieda into the angle of his wrist. He swung her with a simian straight arm a few inches from his body, continuing without pause, with wonder, to describe the clarity of the sounds at night, the lions' roar and the high bark of the seals. My riveting sense was that the baby was a creature alien to him, while his affinity arched over Primrose Hill to the animals. I know that this feeling was not invention on my part, because years later, though I had lost touch with Zulfi, I encountered a description of the moment secondhand, in the account of *Orghast at Persepolis* (the Peter Brook production for which Ted invented a guttural, visceral Esperanto) written by our mutual friend Anthony Smith.

The evening was pleasant, staccato, strained, as such evenings tend to be. I didn't know Sylvia Plath. I remember nothing vivid except that moment and don't know what the situation was between them. I'm a novelist. I make things up — not "out of whole cloth," but out of scraps and ravelings, the motives, tensions, failures, dinners, guests, guilt, babies, bitterness, and blame of lived and watched experience. Oh, yes, with a little license, out of my own quarrel-stunned later years, if I wanted to write a fiction of that evening such as to charge it with everything to come, I could assemble a marital scenario:

The new baby fusses four hours a night, and although he spells her sometimes, it's understood between them that this is her job. She urges him to nap in the daytime as she does. Instead he mounts to his borrowed study: *he must work some time.* She does not work. She bites her tongue: *it's all very well for you.* On Monday last they entertained Jane Truslow and Peter Davison — Peter whom she scalds in her journal but can't turn away — and Monday next she will cook for Ann Davidow whom she adores and her brilliant fiancé Leo Goodman — all four of them Americans showing up on the doorstep out of her past. On Thursday they dined with the Eliots and Spenders, splendidly — they are Ted's admirers. But both of them are exhausted. Late in the pregnancy she wrote home that she had declared a moratorium on visitors. Now she claimed that Ted's writing time was her first priority. But all the same, without so much as a by-your-leave to him — out of that profligate enthusiasm that erupts when she dresses up, when she mixes with celebrity, when she scintillates in her big-gestured way — she has hocked their Saturday too, to chattering hopefuls. And now! she's pent with fury that he's playing Mary to her Martha. Her outburst barely holds till the guests go home. She is molten, and he's stone. It lasts through Frieda's sleep and waking. Hurricane Sylvia paces with the baby in the little living room; he lies listening through the racket to the caged lion and caged owl. Next day, wrung, frightened, they rearrange their promises, their expectations. They reattach, apocalyptically. When Ann and Leo come on Monday they are limp with averted disaster. The dinner is delightful. She says to Leo: *While you're at Cambridge, you must look up this lively American girl.*

What is a matter of record is that Sylvia wrote very little between January and June of 1960, and that when she wrote again she "sizzled in the blue volts" of "The Hanging Man" and mourned the "Stillborn" poems that had "a piggy and a fishy air." She also wrote a short story, "A Day of Success," which Ted later described as a pastiche for a woman's magazine. In this story the husband is a writer but the wife is not. He, having sold a television play, goes off to lunch with a high-powered career woman while she nurses the baby and a daylong jealous fantasy. Much of her angst has to do with makeup and clothes. Plath exploits the "squalidia" of Chalcot Square: inside, the sewing scraps spread around the cramped flat and the husband's borrowed study up steep stairs, outside, the drab houses, the nude trees over which clouds hang sagging their "soiled parachutes." The conclusion brings the husband home with a mortgage contract on a country house, praising the attar of pablum and cod liver oil on the little wife.

These are the motifs of pulp romance — the hulking man, the threatening sexpot, the ascendancy of the plucky domestic mouse. And the story demonstrates what Sandra Gilbert saw in Plath as "on the one hand, a deeply traditional female anxiety that she could not keep up with the elan of the male imagination, and, on the other, a deep *Ladies Home Journal* conviction that she *should* not keep up" — an anxiety not occasioned by anything subtle or subversive in the dynamic of the fifties.

It has to be said this is an odd enterprise — scavenging my attic to research my own juvenilia. Name-dropping is always meant to aggrandize the dropper by proximity to the famous. In his *Contemporary Authors* series autobiography, Peter Davison displayed a like impulse on his wife's behalf: "Jane and Sylvia had lost their fathers and had been sent to Smith College by widowed mothers. They both lived in a scholarship dormitory called Lawrence House, both majored in English, both studied with Alfred Kazin." It takes a light hand to make more point than that. Sandra Gilbert does it deftly in the essay "In Yeats's House," allying herself with Plath as one of those "who share her literary desire if not her destiny."

But the circumstance I am facing now *is* a question of destiny: that so many of us identified not just with the desire but with the four winds of Sylvia's self-judgment — "sloth, fear, vanity, and meekness." That the pretty girl in the boatload of 'brights that went off to England with my boyfriend has become for me, too, the emblem of a generation.

When the Barnard class of 1958 got together for a reunion not long ago, the talk turned from newsy catching-up to bemused excitement that we saw with such a single eye our place in what we had begun to understand as history. The Barnard graduates of ten years later headed out to mend the world. But in 1958 not one of us had heard of "feminism" except to describe antiquated efforts to win the vote. "Liberation" was a word we used for "Europe" and "the Jews." Every one of us remembered some stifled anger at the status quo (for me it had come out my senior year in a play inspired by Milton's misogyny — the Fall told from a woman's point of view), but we all assumed that Mr. Right was a birthright, that we would find and marry him, and that it was important to have an education for our children's sake. Many of us also had professional plans and grand aspirations, but not one of us set out to invent a new status for divorce. We were not designing the alcoholism, depression, or suicide attempts that many of us endured. I remarked how smart and vibrant we now appeared to be after all. A classmate pointed out that only those who feel all right about themselves show up at a reunion.

Sometimes the age ushers forth a couple that perfectly captures its image of romance. The Victorians had the Brownings: female frailty, a repressive patriarch, a dashing savior. For the flapper era it was the Fitzgeralds: great wealth got by guts and chutzpah, punishment by crash and madness. The Hugheses are our Fitzgeralds: shabbier, transnational, postwar. Her ambition had more reach, less glitz. His was to be, not wear, the fox. Ted and Sylvia became our paradigm for the reason that their collision came at the moment before women's liberation gave itself a name. Feminists latched onto Sylvia Plath as the artist eaten alive by the demands of the patriarchal hearth, and onto Ted Hughes as the unreconstructed male: hunter, philanderer, setter of exercises for the little poet-wife, a balker at household and paternal chores, one who took his freedom while she wailed for hers. Hughes's defenders deplored with him that her suicide, together with the brilliance of her poetry, seemed to validate these complaints.

Admirers are reluctant to say that Plath-the-poet attained her status because she killed herself. Other literary suicides — Ernest Hemingway, for macho instance, Anne Sexton for womanly — only make us regretful in an uneasy way. But for Sylvia these two things are true: the *Ariel* poems are stunning, incandescent poems; and she set her seal on them by ending there. The classic cry of the trapped wife at the beginning of the woman's movement was that she was not taken seriously. She was judged melodramatic, hysterical. She was not *heard*. One of my fictional heroines (who decides not all too heroically to live) complains of her husband: "He said I was overstating the case. I think that's very likely. Only I don't know, when people do commit suicide, or have abortions, what words you use for them, not to be offensive."

To a large number of women Sylvia represented not so much a victim as money-where-her-mouth-was. What she forced, like the characters in an existential play, was the making concrete of the metaphor: the end of marriage is a sort of death.

I married a man with a smaller talent than Ted Hughes, and a shorter fuse. When I left him in 1971 and brought my two boys back from England to Illinois, we rented a tidy stone house in a subdivision whose name represented two natural phenomena not present — such as Moutainbrook, or Valleygrove, or Glendown. I went through two months, maybe three, of manic freedom. I scarcely slept; I talked into the night obsessively. I wrote reams, invented television shows, took taxis into the Chicago hinterlands to pitch them to producers. I had telepathic and magical experiences, was full of portents, eerie conjunctions, and general meaning-making. I soon crashed, and when I crashed the garbage gathered in the kitchen and in my head. The effort of feeding the boys and putting them on the school bus could flatten me till they came home at three. I couldn't remember what to do with food. I couldn't read. I could scarcely drag myself from bed, and it's only in retrospect I see the kindness of the fact that, by biological accident, sleep was for me a friend.

My memory of that time is full of holes, blurred by agony and a now-blurred sense of the agony. Dancing with suicide, I read A. Alvarez's disquisition on the subject, *The Savage God*, and had as one odd impulse a fierce refusal to sell my recollections of Sylvia Plath. We were alarmingly short of money, so this had a certain integrity. On the other hand, no one was offering to buy them. Shortly after Sylvia's death, Charles Monteith had told me that she had expected a babysitter but had left the door to the children's room open, the window closed, so that it was somebody else's responsibility whether they survived or not. Eric White of the British Arts Council told me a few years later that Sylvia had meticulously arranged for the children's safety. Now I saw that Alvarez had amassed evidence for this anti-Medea view without divulging where he got it. The poems seemed to say the children would die. I could not imagine harming my own boys, but I could imagine being speculated about and mis- and re- and sentimentally interpreted. Part of my protectiveness was anger that Plath was so famous and I was so obscure. At that point I could write nothing but a journal by turns sluggish and howling:

Looking everywhere for authority, for sanction, an adolescent still, sitting here naked in this wilderness with the upturned smirk of a born teacher's pet . . . Those who have found no way of laughing are uppermost in my mind. Suicide. My looks will go, have been wasted. Can't face, don't want, the time before it gets better. What value to endure? . . . I recognize a creature of the fifties: it doesn't help. If I must be dead or his wife it is better to be his wife, isn't it? No desire to see (not see) my reputation and social significance enhanced in the manner of Sylvia Plath.

Writing of Plath's *Letters Home*, Jo Brans says, "The most consistent tone . . . is bright insincerity." Hughes thought the letters a flimsy mask. But Sylvia did not invent this tone; it is the mode of the letter home. By fluke I have here in this attic stack not only my own but my brother's letters to our parents for the period 1960–71, his on manila newsprint from the copy desks of the *Oakland Tribune*, the *New York Times*, and the *Los Angeles Times*, mine on flimsy blue Belgian airletters and British A4 onionskin. Both his and my missives contain a wonder of information. They list furniture acquisition, debts, job offers, mortgages, raises, reviews, prizes, praises of authority. They record the dates of *partum*, weights of newborns, feeding schedules, colic, first words, first teeth; they place in quotation marks hundreds of adorable sentences. They detail the Christmas presents received, appreciated, worn, and refused-to-be-put-away. They say in several dozen ways, "felt very grand and proud of Ted." They are plucky. They omit. They prevaricate. They lie.

What remains to be said and has scarcely begun to be said is that the men of my generation were traumatized by failed marriage, too. It is not my place to say this at any length or with any force, because I lived the female part in the psychodrama. (*Of course he has a case*, my brother said when I tried to "be fair." *Everyone does. It's not your job to plead it for him.*) Some men were, like Sylvia, abandoned, and some, like me, escaped; but contrary to the perspective that has evolved, few of us, male or female, rebelled against our parents by making commitment optional. On the contrary. Most men of the fifties were equally trapped in the engorged expectations of marital and familial fulfillment. I have talked several male friends through pain they did not think they could outlive. I have known closely over periods of thirty and sixty years respectively, two men who performed as caretakers to mentally disturbed, disturbing wives. What causes such mental imbalance is very much at the center of the issue, but in practical terms these men played the part we assign the wife: they cleaned and cooked, cajoled into calm,

concealed violence, smoothed feathers in all sorts of social relations —
and lied, lied to their families.

We are used to the notion that in order to attain autonomy we must
rupture the family bond into which we were born, though that family
is permanent in our identity. The illusions and restrictions that had
grown up around marriage in the fifties made it for many of us necessary also to wrench and wrest ourselves from the families we had
made. This also became our identity; it does not go away.

Ted and Sylvia, of course, did not divorce. They were the couple
that parted till death did them forever bind, in the grim celebrity that
Hughes rolled before him like Sisyphus's rock for the rest of his life,
and toward which the present piece is a further offering. Condemna-
tion of Hughes was fueled by the suicide of Assia Wevill, for whom he
left Sylvia, the question being: did he drive them to it or was he drawn
to troubled women? Surely the only answer that will serve must en-
compass *both* and *neither. Birthday Letters*, which Hughes published
shortly before his death, both rekindled the controversy and began a
redressing of the balance; and his personal papers, which have been acquired by Emory University, will do so further.

In *Birthday Letters* Hughes reads the portent and the damage of
failed marriage back into that time, reads the viper back into the rag
rug, the coffin lid in the table top. One poem in the collection, "Epiphany," recalls the period of Frieda's infancy in the little flat near the
zoo. Tracking backward the route Sylvia wrote out for me from Chalk
Farm tube station to Chalcot Square, he writes of being a new father,
light-headed with exhaustion, when a young man crossing the bridge
offers him a fox cub for a pound. He hesitates, tempted but also thinking of Sylvia's reaction and the unpredictable power of a fox in their
cramped flat.

The fox is a recurrent image in Hughes's poetry, and serves myriad
purposes. In the famous "Thought-Fox," from the first line it stands
as metaphor for the process of poetic composition. In "Epiphany" the
fox is both vividly present and deeply emblematic as "what tests a marriage." Hughes acknowledges the familiarity, the confrontation, the
fear in the cub's eyes, and then the demands it would grow to make as
an adult. The poet hesitates, then escapes into the Underground "as if
out of my own life," mourning his failure to risk the test that he — and
Sylvia — had been offered.

With or without a new baby in the house, this is an impudent im-practicality at which any wife might roll her eyes. It is also a cry against the loss of self in marriage that any feminist might endorse. The period of blaming Ted Hughes is like the period during a divorce when only anger will fuel the necessary action. Such anger is useful; it is produc-tive. But that isn't the same thing as a whole story. It rejects the truth that for a man, too, the damage of a failed marriage may never heal.

Hughes was aware of the damage. He later wrote to a friend lament-ing his poetic irresolution, describing the early traumas as huge metal doors, shutting on his psyche with such force that, in spite of his suc-cess, his laureateship, his international fame, he had never as a poet been able to penetrate them.

Four months after I had left my husband, in April of 1972, I wrote to reassure my anxious parents:

> I got the job. The offering price is $14,500 instead of $15,000, which I take to represent the fact that I was not at my scintillating best when I was in Tallahassee . . . fair enough. . . . I had a curious, old old reaction to this job offer this morning . . . a kind of embarrass-ment that I have a job and he doesn't. Although I believed or tried to believe that there was no professional jealousy between us, I know that really I always suffered from a fear that I'd succeed pro-fessionally and he wouldn't, and made light of my accomplishments because of it. Perhaps so much so that I eventually made light of them to myself, and so lost a sense of my own work.

Plath sounded a contradiction and crushed it into a few words in the few hours before the children awoke. There is room to wonder, without ascribing to any theory of madness as genius, whether she might have survived had she not drained that last of her energy into those poems, and how she might have plotted out her continuance.

Without suicide, she could not have raised her children on the prof-its of poetry. It is true, as her journals take for axiom, that her earning options in the fifties involved either the stiletto of the career "girl" or the bluestocking of the academic. This was a stark alternative, not a continuum. It would have been hard to foresee the national net-work in place by now, with its full-throated emphasis on nurturance, woman-power, and the workshop. By and large, American writers no longer think they have to be in New York to be serious. The genders, races, idioms, and ethnicities grant one another an equal right to make sentences; they acknowledge a common struggle and common enemies. Sylvia would surely have been tempted back to teach in that university sinecure that opened for writers throughout America in the late sixties and seventies (and is now narrowing again). She might like Zulfi Ghose have ended up at Texas–Austin, or with Jonathan Spence at Yale, or with Katie Stimpson at NYU ("File this crap under *crap*").

In the journals she disparaged the desiccation of old age, poignantly claiming that, "When you're young, you're so self-reliant." If in her case the self-reliance foundered, perhaps her assessment of age was flawed as well.

It's possible. In October of 1998 Sylvia would have achieved retirement age. Imagine her if you will, grayed, still lean but looser-bodied, rising to the podium of the Associated Writing Programs beside Grace Paley, Maxine Kumin (and — why not? — Anne Sexton resurrected, too), freed by her PC of all those arduous retypings, her London flat now central-heated, likewise her suburban pool, the children of her first failed marriage grown and accounted for, she peaceably partnered or peacefully alone like the rest of us at sixty-plus; saying: *it was bloody, but I'm glad they got to me in time.*

Well, it's hard to want. I have been bred to ambivalence. Still, as they say of aging, I don't care for the alternative. Maybe I could invite her down to give a reading in Florida. I'd do spaghetti with bay scallops. I would get to know Sylvia Plath. We would talk about formalism, feminism, the eternal juggling act. I would ask her ideas on the corporate decimation of publishing, on the durability of ambition, the petard of early promise. We might bring down the British woolens still bundled in my attic, slice them up to braid a rag rug. She might by now have granddaughters, even a stepdaughter as I have. We might talk about the persistence of the angst of adolescent girls. Yes, good lord. These teen magazines and this gothic glitter spread around my living room. Think what metaphors she would make of belly piercing or a studded tongue!

Danger and Domesticity in the Deep South . . . .

n August of 1972 I came to Tallahassee, Florida, in search of a gas stove. It was a propitious season for suicide, and I think I had a sense that I had better not muff my chance. My children were in Illinois with their father, who could not know my address because I had none. I knew no one in Tallahassee except, minimally, the gentlemanly gentlemen of the Florida State University English Department, who had hired me under the delusion that I could function as an associate professor. On the flight to the interview I had hoped that my plane would crash, but it had not, and they had offered me the job. So it was to be a stove. The discovery of my body, in some fly-ridden state of neglect, would be shocking to the gentlemen, but hardly a cause for grief on their side, and therefore cause for little guilt on mine.

It was a propitious season for suicide. I had spent the sixties sheltered in an English rose garden, and on the drive south through America I experienced the wastes of Alabama as a wasted state. Unable, at some junction of highway scrub, to bear my solitude, I had hailed into my bulbous station wagon two girl hitchhikers who carried white vinyl purses and wore white socks below miniskirts. They talked waitressing, rape, buggering, and revenge. "I'd like t'get a shotgun and blow 'im away," one said. I thought if they mugged and murdered me it would save me a last apartment hunt, but they did not. They waved cheerily good-bye in Birmingham, and I continued alone to Tallahassee, where Tennessee Street dissected Monroe in a blaze of Exxon, Allstate, Kentucky Fried, and Taco Bell, like a cross burning on a suburban lawn. In the backyard of the house that had been lent me by a vacationing faculty family, a banana tree was rotting into the corner of the pool. The water was tepid oil. The house was infested with fleas, and the shag stank of the chemical that had not killed them; they leapt tenaciously to my ankles in the stink.

It was clear to me that it was a good place to die, but it was not clear to me how anyone could *live* here. What, after all, is *northern Florida*, apart from a contradiction in terms? There was nothing of the north about it, and nothing of Florida, but rolling red earth with a smell of immaculate decay, massive oaks curtained in chigger-ridden moss, pines both thick and stark, and everywhere (except at Monroe and Tennessee) a fecundity of flora that masked infection. The life cycle run amuck.

I hied myself to the Leon County Mental Health Center — in order, I said to myself, to fortify myself for the gas-stove search — where a sensible soul let me practice emotional hemophilia on his carpet for a while, and then advised me to get eight hours solid sleep and three meals a day. For some reason he seemed to understand that although I had been hired at a decent professional salary, I was broke; and the center charged me two dollars for this absurd advice. From this vantage point it seems to say something about Tallahassee: you may arrive dying, but if you go looking for it from a human soul, for two dollars you can get three meals and eight hours of solid sleep.

Nevertheless, I searched diligently for my chosen item of self-demolition; and I credit my failure to the appearance of a number of folk who did not find the season quite propitious for my doing-in. The pest control woman dropped by, for instance, on her own time, to make sure she'd done her job. She was a big woman in coveralls and a bouffant, an infectious drawl: Lord *yas*, she said, fleas *and* divorce; I must feel like the world was turning 'cause I was falling right off of it. She fumed at her failure, fumed the house with lethal gas, and laid the fleas flat. I evacuated the poisoned rooms on her advice, not noticing that this was a life-affirming choice.

The wife of a powerful and prestigious professor (who was not, however, then the department chairman and was therefore not responsible for me) asked me to dinner five nights in a row, with no discernible reason, since neither he nor she had any experience with separation trauma, and no particular reason to intuit my state. I must have been poor company. There was a lot of bourbon, and there were a lot of brownies, homemade. I don't remember what came in between, but

I assume it must have been one of my three meals. "Be sure to lock your car door in town," the pert wife adjured me. "You can't be too careful." I smiled and downed another brownie. I had never locked a car door in my life. They invited a bourbon-loving colleague who advised, "Don't ever offer a student liquor in your home. If they drive drunk, you're responsible for it." I smiled again. I had no home.

In the mall where I had gone to buy shampoo (a life-affirming signal, at this vantage point, if I've ever seen one), a candidate for City Commission grasped my hand and launched into a passionate tirade against the widening of Thomasville Road behind the Los Robles neighborhood. The quality of life, he told me, can't be bought. What was my name? I burst into tears at this combination of dictum and query, which daunted him not for a second. Would I like to contribute to the quality of life in terms of a protected neighborhood? I gave him five of my last fifty dollars and snuffled into Walgreens to wash my hair.

The man who pumped my gas saw my faculty sticker, and talked football. Relationships between town and gown, I had learned in the six previous years of professing, were tenuous and hostile, and in those days FSU was losing humiliatingly. Nevertheless (*five gallons and check the oil, please*) he appropriated and assumed a common ground. Bless them Seminoles, give 'em a chance, eh? What did I think? I thought my water pump was shot. But he thought just the gasket, and fixed it for seven-fifty. C'mon, guys, honest mechanics went out when I was a kid. "Have a nice day," he said, somehow not rote. And I went off to find the stove.

No luck. Apartments were small, tasteless, expensive, and electric; the clapboard houses I could afford were moldering and mildewed; the search became annoying and then obsessive. I complained about it to my evening host, who came up with bourbon, real estate agents, brownies, commiseration, more bourbon, more brownies, and advice. Try the south side, the west side. I was born in the southwest, and I knew the meaning of low-rent. *Northern Florida?*

On the southwest side the manager's wife showed me into a spacious stuccoed room with sliding doors onto a blue tiled pool (*Oh Mom!* said my elder son, Tim, when he arrived. *It's love at first sight*). The jacarandas nodded at the door. There was a bright wall space for the paintings I had shipped (an affirmation?), a dishwasher and a disposal, and a Swiss fern hanging at the porch, which somebody had left behind. She chattered, the ladylike landlady, this most unliberated of women, of children outdoors and practical pediatricians and pet rules and cleaning-women-at-minimum-wage and school buses and Winn-Dixie-versus-Publix. She quite exhausted me with her solicitation. As I signed the contract and wrote a bad check for the deposit in her Hummel-encrusted living room, I remembered that I had not inspected the stove.

It was electric.

I bought a coil-trivet for my Belgian coffee pot, which arrived by Mayflower along with the rest of the paraphernalia of an ongoing life, and I came, by Mayflower, over to the pilgrim's life.

The violent August sky-fire gave way to violent September sky-water. The boys arrived. Classes began. The season muted to a mild sifting of pine needles and leaf-scented balm. Tim and Alex got impetigo and ringworm and chiggers and swimmer's ear. They did not get colds. They did not, more amazingly, get put down for their British accents. They were asked to show and tell on the globe. They were integrated into the heartland of bigotry, along with a local black third grader who pointed out Africa as where *he* came from, and a Saudi Arabian six-year-old who brought etched brass mocha pots to school. We swam in the sinkholes at Thanksgiving and sailed off Alligator Point at Christmas, and I began to concede that if anybody *could* live here, it was probably my children.

More gradually it dawned on me that my students were doing all right too. I was used to seeing intelligence packaged in a blasé English accent with all the commas in the right place. At FSU it came mainly in cutoffs and halter tops, and I was a little slow to recognize it, mainly out of the egotism of my own terror.

For the first six months I passed the gothic towers of the Westcott Building — which had been gutted by fire and showed empty sky behind its upper-story windows like a hallucination by Magritte — in a state of stage fright and pre-exam readiness. I entered the humid, fan-loud basement of the Diffenbaugh Building praying only to get through the hour. And then one day I didn't. As I stood at the lectern in a white linen skirt, my terror burst through in a clean blast of what is medically termed "dysfunctional bleeding." I invented a lie, dismissed the class, and managed to retreat, undiscovered if undignified. This performance was a turning point. I retreated, I bled, but I did not die. I took a week in the hospital, and by the time I got back I had a decent lecture to give them, about Spiro Agnew and the Aristotelian notion of the tragic downfall. They took notes.

I bought a TV set and a car and then a bigger TV set and a smaller car. After two years I bought a brown concrete box of a house because it had two (chigger-ridden) moss-hung oaks in the backyard. Since we had cockroaches we got an Orkin Man, and since we had him we got a cat, and then since we had the fleas anyway we got a dog. The next year we got a bigger dog and a litter of kittens and had to get a bigger house, which we found in an acre of dense pines-and-azalea woods in the middle of town, in the protected neighborhood at the edge of Thomasville Road. I gave another five dollars to the city commissioner and joined the Los Robles Neighborhood Association.

I was not mistaken about Tallahassee. It is a violent town. It has the third highest rape rate in the nation, a dubious distinction. From my classroom window I can see the Chi Omega House, where Theodore Bundy battered those four young women, two to death. One of my own students, a mild-mannered, curly-topped junior, was murdered in a drug deal not far from our first house. One of my colleagues was shot point-blank in the head in his office by a Ph.D. candidate he had failed. Another received in his office mailbox a dead squirrel and a love letter written either in the squirrel's blood or the writer's. Another was called home from our house one night because his babysitter had been raped. One student telephoned politely to excuse himself from class; he had to be with a friend who had been arraigned for setting his grandmother on fire. Another stormed across campus one night so angry at her boyfriend that when a would-be rapist attacked her she belted him in the stomach and sent him running. Another called collect from somewhere in London, she was not sure where, to say she had already swallowed the pills and didn't know how to get to the hospital (she got there). Another evening when I held class at home, the same student ate all the aspirin, Demerol, and Corricidin tablets she could find in my bathroom cabinets (there were not enough) and tried to pitch herself out of the car on the way to the ER. One afternoon I arrived at her house to find her pouring boiling water over her slashed wrists at the kitchen sink, where twenty-four knives were neatly lined up on display.

If, against such a catalog, I tell you that most of us — family, students, neighbors, friends — live in a small-town atmosphere out of
the film-forties, more Jimmy Stewart than John Hinckley, Jr., more
Spanky McFarland than Squeaky Fromme, you may think us naive. If
I tell you we paddle out on plastic rafts in the shark-infested Gulf, if I
set against the general perfidy of the time and clime, no more august a
body than the Los Robles Neighborhood Association, you may think
us irrational. So let me begin by suggesting that the frogs in this town
are crazy too.

We have two. One is a squat toad that has taken up under a dis-
carded sink in the corner of the garage. When I clean he hops only
briefly and minimally away, finds his shelter again as soon as I replace
it. Our predatory cat Shakira spends the night on the hood of the car
four feet above his head. Why the toad prefers this upended enamel
shelter to all the protection of the woods outside I do not know, but I
can only conclude he likes the company.

I would think it superfluous to describe this toad as squat, except
that we have also been chosen, at the kitchen window, by a tree frog
of amazing slenderness and delicacy: long legs arched and minutely
muscled, a luminous white belly pulsing, the slightest membrane also
throbbing at the throat. One night my son Alex caught him, brought
him in, let him hop in the sink, tried to convince him to attach to the
inside of the window, failed, and put him out again. If I were a tree
frog, this trauma would have sent me back to the hinterlands; but the
next night he had sucked himself against the kitchen light. I am going
to put our toad and our frog up for membership in the Los Robles
Neighborhood Association.

Los Robles is Spanish for "The Oaks," though it is locally déclassé to
give it the Spanish pronunciation, and like those from Nawlins, Karo,
and Toosawn, the initiate announces himself by getting it right the first
time: *Loss Rowbulls.*

It is a pie-shaped piece of hilly red jungle-forest set in what was at
one time the outskirts of town, but is by now within walking distance
of the most inskirts mall. At the narrow end of the wedge is The Gate,
which is not a gate, there being no fence, but a two-story arch of ivory
stucco with a red Spanish tile roof. The Gate serves no purpose, except that it is rather handsome in a thirties sort of way, and that "you
can't miss it." We live at the other end along the crust. In between are

a scant two acres of park with venerable moss-hung oaks, several thousand trees, and perhaps a hundred households of people willing to fight fleas, cockroaches, kudzu vine, and ivy. The flora meanders from tropical to temperate and back again; palms in the front yard give way to pines and roses in the back, which abut a fence of honeysuckle that trails over onto a border of monkey grass. For forty-nine weeks of the year the neighborhood is every color of green from gold to black. For three weeks in early spring the dogwoods come out in blinding cumulus; the magnolia, redbud, and wild cherry explode overhead; every anonymous bush turns out to be an azalea and runs amuck in an indecent exposure of scarlet, fuchsia, purple, pink, and mauve. After three weeks, just when the scent and color have begun to cloy, it storms, the flowers fall, and the streets retreat to green again.

The neighborhood is "protected," of course, only in the sense that you can't cut down the hundred-and-fifty-year-old oaks that grace its minuscule park, and that if you wanted to put a McDonald's on Ponce Street (*Pawnse Stritt*), you would have the Association to deal with. During World War II even this sort of protection broke down, the zoning rules got set aside, and a number of modest shingle-fronted bungalows were built that are now rented to students and sold to people of unpretentious income; these inhabitants tend to be the fiercest of the Association's protectors.

On the other hand, we don't seem to be the target for violent crime that our geographical position would suggest. I think we are protected by our erratic hours and ages — the retired, the professional, the professorial, and the undergraduate, whose cars go in and out all day and whose toddlers are even now messing in the azalea bed of the late savings and loan vice president. Anyway, we are odd acquirers, and I suspect that the thieves are clever enough to suspect that our most valuable stuff couldn't be recognized or dealt with: a Sumi scroll from eighteenth-century Japan; somebody's grandmother's hand-painted Limoges hot-chocolate pot; a Persian rug that actually came from the place called Persia in the days when it was still called Persia. Where antiques are much valued, the video equipment is likely to be on the ancient side as well, and I suppose we don't cut much ice with the local fence.

We are so old-fashioned that we have not yet got round to the generation gap, and the octogenarians on their Sunday stroll can be seen shrugging at the drift and waft of pot, heard reminding each other that times change. We are so old-fashioned that the newly-marrieds drop in on the old widowers to make sure they've got bread and transport. We have a village witch who will not let the schoolkids cut through her cactus patch and calls the cops every time a dog barks, but she flies in and out on her jet broomstick to a more expensive house somewhere else, and is therefore not a proper member of the community. This augments the solidarity among the rest of us. Besides, the cops like to stop by. They have a cup of coffee and a slice of fresh fig cake and tell us the dog can't bark because there's a city ordinance, and we say we'll take care of it, and they go back to the Frenchtown beat.

Once a year, the Association gathers to clean up The Gate, haul fallen boughs, and trim the striplings. Once a year we gather to plant a new dogwood or holly tree. Once a year we hold a rummage sale in the park: attic and basement castoffs come out, the wicker sofas and over-stuffed chairs are set up under the oaks like a green living room. Some-one brings apple dolls, and somebody has made jewelry boxes with metal tops etched in crab and sand dollar shapes. Some of the stuff finds its way out of the neighborhood, but more is bought or bartered from friend to friend: my grandmother's chandelier for your Nikon, my homemade hot pads for your coffee mugs.

The real event is the annual Frolic in the Park. Yes, it is called a frolic, and some of us wear frocks, though the cutoffs and halter tops are in equal evidence. Patchwork quilts and afghans are spread under the trees, the beer keg is packed in ice in a washtub, twenty-four feet of table are laden with ham and chicken and Swedish dill-soaked cucumbers and German shrimp croquettes; there are broccoli pots, smothered onions, marinated pintos, black-eyed peas, peach chiffon pies, deep-dish pecan, demon fudge cakes, and banana walnut breads. Rachel Stowell whispers from blanket to blanket, inviting everybody to her daddy's surprise birthday party. Bob Horniday shouts at a table-ful of adolescents that he doesn't want to see *anybody* under twenty-five in a *chair*. My son Tim arrives in the ancient MG for which he has mort-gaged his young soul, drawing by the hand a gentle Alabaman blonde who is expert on the oboe and the baton. A four-year-old with a greasy fistful of the Colonel's Kentucky Fried pitches fist-first into the gray gabardine skirt of a lady in a matching chignon. The child's mother is as mortified, the lady as gracious, as each might have been in a novel by Henry James. The city commissioner arrives in khaki shorts and a screaming yellow T-shirt emblazoned in a red motto that looks, from my position near the keg, like HOT 'N' JUICY. The commissioner is given a tour of the ancient oaks, shown the foundations of the old blacksmith shop and the scar where the blacksmith tied the horses to be shod. He is shown a patch of mite disease on one venerable tree, a sap-bleeding wound where another was trimmed but not tarred. He solemnly promises to take it up with the city, and joins the volleyball.

When I was a child in Arizona it was like this: the neighbors watered each other's lawns, they checked on the old folks and borrowed cups of sugar. The most terrible thing that happened when I was a child on Alvarado Street was that somebody turned off the main fuse switch when they went on vacation, and left a freezer full of venison. When they came home they carted the spoils to the curb. It was not garbage day, and for twenty-four hours the neighborhood was scandalized by the sweet stench of rotting flesh. There was a plague of flies. Somebody called the cops.

Here, last year, my student Patricia volunteered to keep her parents' motel while they went on vacation. The slight, shy woman from Illinois who checked in at 3:00 A.M. paid for a week in advance by credit card, and Patricia did not discover her suicide until it announced itself in the sweet stench. She, also, called the cops. She said the thing she couldn't get out of her mind, when she finally unlocked the door, was the astonishing number and activity of the flies.

Last week at 1:00 A.M. in a murderous rainstorm, a drunk legionnaire drove over the curb at the bottom of our street, floated into twelve feet of water, and drowned in the duck pond. His four passengers — one of them in her sixties — dog-paddled to the surface, and survived.

We went down to feed the ducks this morning. They scolded each other over the pancake tearings and the rye heels. There are newly hatched goslings, and we kept our distance from the hissing geese. A toddler in a red tank top ran after a mallard who screamed and pitched himself beak foremost into the scummy water. The toddler clapped her hands and turned for kudos to her parents, who were necking on the bank.

The ducks surrounded our feet, but the seagulls whipped overhead and at shoulder height; they screamed and wheeled after the crumbs, neatly catching them in midair. A young man, older than the boy but with a boy's blond cowlick at the crown, stopped to watch us fling our scraps to the gulls, drop them to the ducks.

"I hate these seagulls," he announced. "I wanna get a twelve-gauge shotgun and blow 'em outta the air."

This boy-man had, for instance, no tattoo. He was thin, a little weedy. He had a lazy cocker spaniel at the end of a thin leather leash. I hesitated, then lofted a bit of biscuit toward a cawing gull.

"Let 'em go back where they belong," he gritted through his teeth, and ambled on.

Where the car strayed into the pond, there is not even a commemorative crush of grass.

I came here at thirty-six with the intention of dying, and I suppose I will die here — at ninety or thereabouts, under the third patchwork quilt from the one I am making now, with my great-grandchildren gathered about me to hear the disposition of the chandeliers and the chocolate pots.

I will be a cantankerous old woman, having survived so much. I will tease them on my deathbed, having had my humor and my irony restored by so many years as a member of the Loss Rowbulls Neighborhood Association.

Well, I will tell them: lock the car doors and turn off the gas. Ordinary life is more dangerous than war because *nobody* survives. You gotta lose, but an azalea bush in the hand is just two frogs short of safe and sound.

I don't expect them to be mystified.

Embalming Mom

"I want to put you in a story," I say. "Apparently it's a matter of some importance."

She is ironing and her back is to me. She says nothing and does not turn around, but she licks her finger to test the iron. Her spit sizzles like bacon and I can see her hand. Long strong fingers, violet veins, amber freckles. Under the taut freckled flesh of her forearms her narrow bones roll with the maneuvering of the iron.

"I don't mean professional importance," I say, "but psychological. Spiritual, if you like." She rolls the iron along the board.

Things have not been going too well with me lately — a number of breakages, and not all of them for the first time. The compressor on the air conditioner broke down again. The left earpiece of my reading glasses split at the hinge and I can't see to tape it together without my glasses on. Both of my teenaged sons had their hair cut again, for opposing reasons. I got divorced again, and moved again, or at least, I must not have moved, since I live in the same house in Florida, but it seems to feel as if I have moved again.

She rolls the iron along the board, wide end to narrow end in a serpentine path from her belly toward the window sill. It occurs to me that nobody ever sees her own bones, and that she has therefore never seen these bones that twist and roll under her skin, the forearm bones of a bony woman, their mineral and marrow.

"Well," I say, "important to my soul, if you want to put it that way."

"Hmmph," she says. Does she say, "Hmmph?" It seems unlikely. Perhaps what she says is, "Hah!" I think she sighs. Once my brother Bud pointed out to me that when things fall apart you always run home to Mom. He pointed this out because I was fleeing a threatening lover (again) and he thought I wasn't very well hidden in the breakfast bay. But I told him safety is not the point; the point is feeling safe.

She is ironing the skirt of the pima cotton dress with the white and purple pansies, the pin-tucked yoke, the puffed sleeves edged in eyelet. The pansies part at the point of the iron, swirl left and right under the heel of her hand and wheel down the board behind the butt of the iron. I do not, however, say "butt" in her presence. That much is clear.

I cross my legs, sitting at the breakfast bay, which is covered in some orange substance, a precursor of Naugahyde. I am wearing the trouser suit made out of handwoven amber tweed that I bought off the bolt in Galway at an Incredible Bargain. The trouser suit was stolen out of a parked station wagon in New York in 1972, but it is apparently important that I should be wearing it now, partly because it was such a bargain and partly because I designed and made it myself. I feel good in it: cordial, cool. I think of something I can pass on to her. I laugh.

"Do you know what a friend of mine said the other day?" Cordially rhetorical. "He said: Hell is the place where you have to work out all the relationships you couldn't work out in life."

It's all right to say hell in this context, not as a swear word but as an acknowledgment of a possible place. My mother's not narrow-minded about the nature of hell. I laugh again, and so although she laughs I don't know if she laughs with me; I miss the tone of her laugh. "Haw, haw!"? I hope it's that one, the swashbuckling one.

"I'd rather work this one out here," I say, but am conscious that I mumble and am not surprised that there is no response. I am sitting on the orange plastic of the nook in the bay window, which my father designed and made, watching my mother at the ironing board that folds up into the wall behind an aluminum door. This also was designed and made by my father, who is not here because he is living in the mountains with his second wife although he was true to my mother right up to the end. And beyond. Outside the desert sun slants through the oleanders, illuminating minute veins in the fuchsia petals. The pansies on the ironing board I remember wearing in the sandbox under the oleanders before I started school, which means that my mother is about thirty-five. I am forty-five and three months by the calendar on the window sill to the left of my typewriter.

"What friend was that?" she asks, eventually, with a palpable absence of malice and a clear implication that any friend who goes under the designation "he" is suspect. It was all right to say "hell" but not "he."

"Nobody in particular; just a friend."

"Your father gets sweeter every day," I think she says, and I am sure that her head angles to one side, a long neck made longer by the tight poodle cut of her hair, already graying, already thinning, the corrugations of her neck where it arches no wider than those on the spine of a hardbound book.

"Yes," I say. "Well." She takes the edge of one puff and twirls the eyelet, arching the iron into each semicircle on the board, expertly smoothing it so that when she releases it each arch buoys into a perfect wave. It occurs to me that I can do this, too.

"You know, I'm not sure I feel too well," she says, as if surprised, mumbling now, but she is an old hand at the audible mumble, and I will not rise to it.

Instead I say, "All we need to do is embark on a minor conflict. Anything will do, any of the old ones. My posture, for instance, or the state of my room. Smoking will do. Or that my hair needs cutting."

My elder son has joined the army and writes that he has had his hair cropped; it never occurred to me before that a crewcut makes one a member of a crew. My younger son has scissored his blond thatch so short that it also seems to have erupted out of World War II, but for him it has an altogether different ideological significance. He does not, however, want it called punk. I am so anxious he should like me that I pay to have his left ear pierced and offer him a diamond-chip stud of which I have lost the mate. He accepts it cheerfully, but most days he wears a diaper pin through the punctured lobe.

She deals with the eyelet of the other sleeve, and she turns to me. I am so startled by this success that I reach into my Italian handbag for a cigarette, and my glance catches no higher than the hand she splays protectively over her stomach; I concentrate on the lighting of my cigarette, and can only suppose the shape of her mouth, narrow-lipped but open wide in the narrow-lipped friendly "hah" shape, large straight teeth except for the crossing of the two lower incisors that I encounter in my own mirror every day of my life. I hear her say, nasal on the vowels, "I just don't want you to be indis*creet*, sissy."

This confusingly hits home. I recognize the authenticity of it — the plaint, the manipulation, but also the authenticity. Because I am indiscreet; it is my central fault. I confess to freshman students, junior colleagues, anyone with a dog smaller than a breadbox. I expose myself by telephone and telegraph; I say it with ink. I betray the secrets of my friends, believing I am presenting their cases. I embarrass clerks in the Kmart.

But she has her back to me again, and all I can see is the parting of the pin-tucks left and right as she deftly presses them away from the pearl shank buttons. Because she didn't mean the right thing and has no notion that she has hit home.

"What does that mean, indiscreet?" I ask, a little shrill, so that I deliberately draw the smoke in after I've said it, feeling the depth of my lungs, my verbal bottom. "Do you mean sex? Do you mean: lie better?"

"I'm not going to be sidetracked into a discussion of words," my mother says, a thing she would never say.

"It's not a sidetrack," I nevertheless reply. Her forefinger sizzles.

I need an ashtray. I know there are no ashtrays here, but I'm willing to choose carefully among the things I know are here: the amethyst-glass pot with calico flowers set in paraffin; the Carnival glass cup with her name, "Alma," etched in primitive cursive; the California Fiesta pottery in the lurid colors of the zinnias along the front walk. I cross to the cupboard and take the little Depression glass fishbowl because I know it best, because it currently houses a tiny goldfish on the window sill to the left of my typewriter in my house in Florida.

"It's true that I'm indiscreet," I confess, indiscreetly, "but it's not entirely a fault." I tap my ash, and my hair prickles hot against my turtleneck. Both of my husbands liked my hair long, although the second one did not smoke and the first blamed me for indiscretion. The convolutions of authority are confusing. "It's also simply the way I am; it's a negative side of my strength. The thing I want most of all is an understanding audience, a teaching one. The best thing is to tell and be understood. Do you understand?"

"I've never looked at any man but your father," she replies, to the oleanders, to the waffle iron, to the piqué collar that she designed and made and that she now parts into two perfect eyelet-edged arches of Peter Pan.

"*Mama!*"

No, that won't do. I must not put myself in the hysterical stance because if anything is clear, the clear thing is that she is the hysterical one and I'm the one who copes, deals, functions, and controls. I am the world traveler, the success.

I continue in a more successful tone. "We could start with Dad if you like, but I don't think it's the best place because it's so hard to be honest."

"I *hope* I brought you up to be honest!" Back to me still, she whips the dress from the board and holds it up for her own inspection.

"I mean that there are so many ways of lying apart from words, especially where marriage is concerned. I think it would be better if we just kept it between you and me."

"There's lying and there's telling the truth, especially where marriage is concerned!"

This strikes a false note. She is not speaking to me as she must speak to me because I am not speaking to her as I must speak to her. I tap my ash into the fish bowl while she takes a copper wire hanger and buttons the now-perfect dress onto it at the nape. With one hand she holds the hook and with the thumb of the other she flicks one neat flick at the button while index and middle finger spread the hand-bound buttonhole and the button pops into place. I can see the gesture with magical clarity; I can do it myself. Once when I was caught playing doctor in the tamaracks with crippled Walter Wesch, she sat me in the basin and spread my pink bald mons veneris with the same two fingers, soaping with the flick of her thumb, scourging me with her tongue in terms of Jesus and germs.

"Mama, look," I say, "the reason I want to do this — try to understand — is that I *want* to tell the truth. I want to capture you . . . as you really are." I squirm on the plastic, hair hot at the nape, and add despairingly, "As a *person*."

Does she say, "Hah!"?

"I've tried before, and you came out distorted. I know you're remarkable . . ."

Now she is doing one of Daddy's Arrow shirts, a plain white one with a narrow stitched collar. The point of the iron faces one point of the collar, then the other. The long strong far hand stretches against the stitching so the hot collar lies perfectly flat without any of the tiny corrugations that even a laundry leaves these days. I can do this. My two sons can do it.

She turns again, one eyebrow raised and a mocking smile, "What, then, am I the most unforgettable character you've met?"

Not like her, neither the eyebrow nor the words, which have the cadence of a British education. I'm the one with the British education. I try again. She turns back like the film run backward, the point of the iron faces one point of the collar, then the other, she stretches with the strong far hand, the bones of which she has never seen, and turns again robotlike, profile gashed with a smile. "Honey, write for the *masses*. People need to *escape*. They need to *laugh*."

This is closer. My fist is too big to go in the goldfish bowl, and I have no way to stub out my cigarette. I have to hold it while it burns down to the filter and out. So it turns out to be me who says brightly, "Okay, why don't I do you up as 'The Most Unforgettable Character I've Met'?"

To which, against my will, try as I might, she replies, "Why me? Hah, hah, there are plenty of fish in the sea."

"No!" I slam the bowl down dangerously, but it doesn't break. How could it, when it houses the goldfish next to the calendar on the window sill? Dangerously shrill, I say, "That's exactly what I don't want you to say!"

She hands me a shirt out of the basket, a blue one with the same narrow Arrow collar; I understand that I'm supposed to sprinkle it. I fetch a pan from under the stove and fill it with warm water, holding the hot cigarette filter in the hand that turns on the tap. I run water over the filter, which sizzles, and reach for the garbage bin under the sink, ashamed because my back is to her now and I am doing this in full view. The bin is of the step-on sort, chrome lid on a white cylinder adorned with a bow-tied posy of photographically exact nasturtiums. *Nasty urchums*, Bud and I used to call them in the sandbox years, though I don't remember if we dared to say this in front of Mama. I toss the cigarette in the bin and, when the lid slams, curb the impulse to take the garbage out.

My last love affair was trashed over the question of taking out the garbage. It's a common story. He said, "What can I do to help?" and I said, "Thanks, I'd appreciate it if you took out the garbage." He said, "It makes no sense to take it out now; it isn't full. Do you want the sausage sliced or mashed?" I did not want the sausage sliced or mashed, and said so in no uncertain terms. He said, "What are you on about?"

And I was, I admit, a trifle eloquent; it's my job. I put myself in the hysterical stance and he put himself in the imperturbable stance, but it was he who slammed out and that was that. It's common. My mother used to say: common as an old shoe. She meant it for praise, of people who didn't stand on their dignity.

I carry the pan back to the table. "D'you remember when Bud came up with the phrase, 'Mama's Homey Canned Platitudes'?"

At this she swashbuckles; the whole haw-haw comes out and I can hear it from the bottom of her lungs but cannot look at her again because she misses the point; she can laugh at herself but she doesn't know there was real grief in it for us, Bud and me, to whom honesty comes so hard except for money. All I can look at is the linoleum, which is annoyingly and irrelevantly clear, the black outlines of rectangles on a flecked gray ground, the absurdly marbled feather shapes at the upper left corner of each rectangle: it is not the linoleum I want to see.

"Look, you don't understand," I stumble, splashing points of warm water from the pan to the shirt on the table, each spot an instant deeper blue as if I were splashing paint. "The point is that it's become a kind of platitude for us, Bud and me. It's easy to remember your clichés, but they prevent us from remembering you; they only conceal something we never saw because we were kids and kids have to . . . see . . ."

The telephone rings rescuingly. She crosses from the ironing board to the phone, which she pulls through the little sliding door that my dad designed and made so that it, the phone, can be both reached from and closed into both the kitchen and the den; she answers, "Hello?" and swashbuckles the laugh. How can it be that the laugh is false and the pleasure genuine? Can I do this myself? "Why, Lloyd!"

It's the preacher, then. As she stands at the telephone I notice what she wears, which is a green cotton cap-sleeved house smock edged in black piping, sent her one Christmas by Uncle Jack and Aunt Louellen and which has, machine embroidered over the flat left breast, a black poodle dog with a rhinestone stud for an eye. I can see this though her back is to me, and I can see the sharp shadow of the wingblades underneath the cotton, the bones she has never seen. I cannot see her face.

"Lloyd Gruber, how nice of you to call! Oh, as well as can be expected for an old lady, haw haw. Yes, she's home, fat and sassy; you know she's got another book out and she's on a *tour*, well, I wouldn't want to tell you I'd pass it around in the Women's Society for Christian

Service but you know it's *those* words that sell nowadays. What? Oh, no, that broke up ages ago. Why, Lloyd, I'm not in the least bit worried about her; you know I was twenty-three myself before I married, yes I was, she's a spring chicken . . ."

"*Mama!*"

Discouragement appears on me as wrinkles in the elbows of Galway tweed. My mother can embarrass clerks in Kress's five-and-dime. I leave the rolled shirt on the table and escape to the dining room where I watch, in the eight thousand prisms of the glass brick window, eight thousand miniature distortions of the sterile orange tree outside, a bough bobbing under the weight of its puckered fruit. I can taste the acrid taste of these oranges from the time Bud tricked me into lagging a tongue across the wet pebbles of their useless flesh. I think I have changed my mind. I think I will simply cross the living room and thread my way down between the zinnias that line the walk . . .

But there she is, crossing toward the living room herself, with the dress and the shirt flapping from the hooks over her hand. She is there, of course, because she is the pushmi-pullyu of the psychic Midlands. If I go to touch her she will recoil, but if I walk away she will be at my heels. I can do this, too. Somewhere are two teenaged boys and a half a dozen former husbands and lovers who will attest that I can do it, too.

She has hooked the hangers on the knob of the corner cupboard to inspect a possible inch of misturned eyelet, a possible crease in the French seam of the Arrow armhole. She says, "Now *what* it is you want, honey?"

Home is the place where, when you have to go there, they don't understand why you've come.

"I want to put you in a story," I say evenly.

Back to me, she presses a hand over her stomach, she makes a little clucking sound of pain, her back arches in the instinctive position of a Martha Graham contraction and releases, rolling upward from the flat buttocks that I do not mention in her presence. I will not mention Martha Graham, Martha Quest, Billy Graham, Billy Pilgrim, Janet Pilgrim. I may mention graham crackers.

"Sissy, I don't want to fight with you."

"Not a real fight, mom. That's just a device to get us started. What I really wanted to do is catch your essential . . ."

The ironing has apparently passed muster because she picks up the hangers again and carries on through the living room. The threadbare grape-cluster pattern of the carpet passes before my eyes, the inset knickknack shelf that my father made, the gilded miniature watering can that I broke on the way home from the fourth-grade hobby fair and lied about; the big blond console TV that can't have appeared before I was in high school; the bookcase with *Hurlbut's Stories of the Bible* and the complete works of Edgar Guest. I follow at her heels, black patent Cuban heels, from which emerge the graceful corrugations of the quadruple-A ankles she is so proud of and of which, having the same ankles in spite of my big bone structure, I am so proud. We pass the bulbous, sagging couch, the oversized chartreuse fronds and magenta flowers on the slipcovers that she produced in an awesome lapse of taste, the impossible flowers into which I flung my hot face on the occasion of my first heartbreak: Ace Johnson, yearbook editor, senior class councillor, and jilt. My face sizzles in the flowers as she pronounces the phrases of impossible misunderstanding: "Why, sissy, cheer up, haw haw, there'll be another one along in a minute; there are plenty of fish in the sea."

My elder son is on a transport ship, seeking discipline and the romance of camaraderie. My younger son is the lead singer in a band called Beloved Children, which plays in bars he is legally too young to enter. I am on occasion invited to hear this group, and I do. I sit wondering at the sweet demonic presence of these children, who wail a noise that I like and envy. As a girl I knew nothing better to do than sit a sizzling wallflower and pray that someone would ask me to dance. The Beloved Children crop their heads and embrace freakdom. One of their lyrics praises masturbation, "the central occupation, generation to generation," but they do not have the courage of their erections because one by one the members of the band come by to warn me that I will be shocked. To which generation do they think I belong? I politely assure them that I can take it.

Now we are into the hall, the cupboard where the Bible and the Ansco camera are kept, the laundry cupboard that my father designed so you could put the clothes in from the bathroom or the hall and which we called a chute though nothing chutes from anywhere to anywhere.

"Let me tell you about something," I say, hurrying after her. The trouser suit is an insane thing to be wearing in this heat, long sleeved and cuffed, lined and turtled at the neck. My hot hair prickles; I was thirty-four and living in England before I had the courage to assert that I would wear my hair straight and long. "Once I went back to a house I'd lived in years before. Not this house, you understand, some other house. I went back, and it hadn't been sold, the real estate market was bad, and it was a white elephant of a house, so it was being rented, and a lot of my old things were still there. I went in, the tenant was very nice, and we fell into conversation, and I lit a cigarette . . ."

I wish I hadn't got into this. I remember the first time she caught me with a cigarette, she and Daddy together, and Daddy said, "Aha! Caughtcha!" but Mama said, "You're trying to kill me!" She hangs the dress and shirt, both, in the long closet with the sliding doors, which makes a kind of sense because when I was five this was my room, but later it was hers and Daddy's, and I see from the set of her shoulders that she has drawn in her chin, but I don't know if it's because I mentioned a cigarette or not.

"He set an ashtray in front of me. It was a cheap, simple, glass ashtray in the shape of a spade, like the ace of spades."

She probes her stomach again. I think she sighs again.

"I'd bought a set of those ashtrays in a little country market some dozen years before and I had used them daily for — what? — four or five years; and in the intervening time I had not thought of them once, they did not form any part of my memory. When he set this one down I flicked my ash in it, and I recognized the way the cigarette sounded on the edge of the glass."

She is at the bureau with her back to me, her face averted even from the round rimless mirror, and she begins to lay out things from the drawer, as if for my inspection: the ebony-handled nail buffer, the little pot of waxy rouge that I once stole and lied about, the porcelain doll that sits now on the sill to the left of my typewriter in my house in Florida.

"I was flooded with a whole sense of the reality of that house, and of my life there. I know I'm not explaining myself very well." And I'm not, but I'm not going to make any reference to Proust. "I was homesick, Mama."

She slides the nail buffer along the bureau top toward the window sill where the oleanders nod. The milk of the oleander leaves is poison, Bud and I were taught, as I later taught my boys that the pods of the laburnum were poison, in the garden of the English house that held the glass spade ashtray.

"There's a story," I blurt, inspired, "by John Cheever. In which one of the characters says that fifty percent of the people in the world are homesick all the time."

"Which marriage was that?" she asks, and smiles at me in the mirror while she is putting on her vermilion lipstick so that her mouth is stretched and distorted over the cartilage and the bones.

"Which marriage was what?"

"In that house." She takes out the powder box decorated in peach-colored feathers and opens it in a minor explosion of peach-colored ash, arranges it in front of the buffer, the pot, the doll on my window sill beside the calendar and the goldfish. It was indiscreet to use a name she doesn't know. I could have quoted Edgar Guest, how it takes a heap o' livin' to be homesick all the time. I should have said that Jesus said life is one long longing to go home.

"Which marriage was it in that house?"

"My first. Look, what I'm trying to say . . . Mama, sometimes — usually when I'm driving, for some reason — I think about something that has happened in my life, good or bad, and I think, *I can't wait to tell Mom*, or else I think, *I can't tell Mom* . . .

"And then," I say, "it's like waking up from a dream, a good dream or a nightmare, the sadness or the relief. Do you understand?"

Facing herself in the mirror she places a finger on her nose and deforms it slightly to the right while with the index finger of her same hand pressing downward and the other index finger pressing upward, she produces from her pores several dozen live curling worms of ivory colored wax. I avert my eyes in the old embarrassment and then in the old fascination focus again on the one specific section of the mirror where she places a finger of the other hand on her nose and deforms it slightly to the left. Everyone who grew up in America in the fifties can do this, too.

"*Will* you understand?"

She takes the puff and dabs the peach-colored ash over her nose and cheeks. Minute clogs of powder catch in the emptied pores. She smiles at herself in the mirror, chin tilted, a smile for the PTA or the Women's Society for Christian Service, and as I avert my eyes in the old embarrassment she says, nasal on the vowels, "All I want is your happiness, sissy."

I put my head in my hands. Through my fingers I can see the knees of my trouser suit, baggy and crushed, with the stains of crushed grass on them. My hair is hot and heavy. I will confess to her. I confess, "Nobody knows better than I do how hard it is to make words say what you mean. But it's taken me all these years to know it was just as hard for you."

"All I *ever* wanted was your happiness," she says for the PTA.

"It's not so!" I adjust my tone and say more successfully, "It isn't so." I go to her and try to take her insubstantial shoulders, try to force her toward the mirror and the crossed lower incisors, but am uncertain whether I see her grimace or mine, the powder in her pores or mine. "You wanted me to be happy your way, by your rules: don't smoke, don't wear pink with red, marriage is sacred, the wages of sin. . . . And the truth is you were holding onto a bunch of phrases just like me. You knew they didn't work. The truth is . . ."

The truth is that my elder son is a romantic militarist and my younger a punk rocker. I laugh to my friends: I don't know where they came from! But I know at least one place they are headed, somewhere years hence, to seek for themselves why they are so much, and so threateningly, me.

"Mommy isn't feeling very well, dear. I think the old ulcer is acting up again."

"Don't go to bed. Please don't go to bed."

But she is out of the smock, which she hangs on the brass hook over the shelf of the shoes. She raises a modest and protective hand to her collar bone above the peach satin slip, over the rosily mottled V of flesh below the collar bone she has never seen.

"Don't go to bed!" I say. "It doesn't fool me, I can do it, too. It's a way of getting what you want without asking for it; you've got ulcers and high blood pressure and adrenaline flux, I've got a fibrolated coccyx and chronic otitis and atopic dermatitis; it doesn't fool me, Mama. I can do it, too."

But I notice that my trouser suit is also gone; it has disappeared from my body as abruptly as it disappeared from the parked station wagon in New York in 1972. I am standing in nothing but my ivory satin teddy. My hand goes to my collar bone and the mottled V of flesh. She reaches into her end of the closet for the polished cotton housecoat in stripes of pink and gray sent her one Christmas by Uncle Jack and Aunt Louellen; she sizzles the zipper up, and I reach into my —

later Daddy's — end of the closet for the puffed-sleeved pansy dress, which I disengage from the hanger with a deft flick of my thumb at the button at the nape and of course it does not fit; it binds at the armholes and the breast, its handstitched hem is above my knees; and yet, it fits so much better than it ought; the time is out of joint.

"Would you get me some milk, sweetie? Funny thing, I always hated milk, and now it's the one thing I can have for my ulcer."

"Don't go to bed."

But she slips under the rose chenille bedspread and lays her tight poodle cut back on the pillow, producing minute wrinkles in the perfectly ironed pink pillowcase, smiling with eyes closed, arms folded over her flat breast. I pull the puffed footstool to her and sit clumsily, crushing the pima pansies as I try to cover my knees, which are stained with grass and tamarack.

"There'll be a brighter day tomorrow," I am almost sure she says. On the nightstand is the photo of her taken on the morning of her wedding day, which now sits beside the doll in my house in Florida. Distractedly I tap my ash; the goldfish attacks it for food. In the photograph she stands beside a mirror in a simple twenties shift of pintucked chiffon, her hair marcelled into a shelf so that the profile is half obscured and the mirror image is full-faced, the strand of pearls breaking over the collar bones, the mouth pensive and provocative, the eyes deeply sad. Daddy used to call them bedroom eyes.

"Mama, look at me."

"Sissy, let me tell you, there are so many people in the world worse off than we are."

"Oh, Jesus, Mama, the starving in China, the man who had no feet."

"Don't take the name of the Lord in vain."

"It's the way I talk, for God's sake."

"No child of mine ever talked that way!"

"Don't be an ass, Mama, it's only words."

"I'll wash your mouth out for you!"

"Will you, will you?"

"It kills me to hear you talk that way."

"Does it? Then let me give you something to wash out of my mouth. Daddy's remarried. He's married again!"

Her eyes have been fluttering and slit, but now they open. I have got her now. She glances away and back, her smile parts on the gash of the crossed incisors.

"There are plenty of fish in the sea, haw haw!" I say.

She says, eyes averted, "Your daddy gets sweeter every day."

"Jesus Christ, don't you understand anything? I saw your bones!"

The pima dress is wrinkled, sweaty, and has sand in the pockets. It will have to be washed again, and ironed again. The compressor on the air conditioner will have to be replaced again. "We carried your ashes up to the top of Marble Mountain, Daddy and I; we flung them over the quarry and the foundations of the house you lived in, over the roof of the general store. And do you know, Mama, they're rubble, the marrow looks like dry dog food. I saw the mineral in your bones, blue melted mineral in the chunks!"

Now her eyes widen, the melted hazel and amber of her eyes speak terror, and I know that mine will do this, too.

"We scattered them, Daddy and I!"

"You're trying to kill me," I know she says.

"No!" I grip both her long strong hands in my own. "No, I'm trying to keep you!" I finger the veins and freckles, feel for the bones of her hands and see my own hands long and strong on the black bones of the typewriter keys. I avert my eyes. Beyond the calendar — the fish, the doll, the photo of her bedroom eyes — tropical sun slants through the azaleas, outlining the veins in their fuchsia petals. I hold her eyes.

"Let me see you, Mama!"

But the hands go limp in mine and the eyes begin to close. The lids are delicately veined. I grip her hands. "I've got you now!"

"Not altogether so," my mother says.

A thing she never would say.

Her hair is blued, purpled, and her pores have disappeared. There is an odor of pansies, oleanders, roses, orange blossoms, peach. The planes of her face have been expertly ironed. All the wrinkles of her cheeks are gone, and her mouth, closed, seems fuller in repose. Deep buttoning makes symmetrical creases in the rose satin on the coffin lid. The people passing speak of her; they say: *dear soul*, and *always cheerful*, and *devoted wife and mother*, and *a lady*. Her hands, crossed, are delicate and smooth. There is about her a waxen beatitude.

I don't know how they do this, but everybody says it is an art. Everybody says they have done a splendid job. They have caught her exactly, everybody says.

Footprints

t's a windy spring Saturday in Savannah, which means that the sharp smell of paper mill comes at you from every corner. Half a dozen of us are headed, pleasantly overfull of shellfish and Molson's ale, from the river to this afternoon's fiction reading at the Associated Writing Program's conference at the Hilton. The AWP convention is probably more like other conventions than it isn't, with the usual complement of business achieved, ideas exchanged, ambition, backbiting, laughter, drink, and sex; but its three hundred or so members are maybe more than usually spirited, and we share an underlying sense of double dislocation: being writers who teach writing, we are slightly at odds with the literary world because we teach, slightly at odds with the academic world because we write. This makes for quick friendships.

Our lunch group contains two novelists, one poet, three of us who are both, and one (me) who is hobbling over the worn bricks on account of a plantar wart removal on my left foot. We pause to admire the old houses — this brass knocker, that iron grillwork — casually regroup, and wander on. Huge David from Alaska ponders whether it would be sanitation or vandalism to pick up the warped wooden sign leaning against the fence, which says "Scottsville Baptist Church" in chipped and fading script. We pass a ramshackle clapboard house half the size of a city block, which looks as if it would fall at the first push of an index finger, but is mounted on two truck beds ready to be moved. One of the Florida novelists remarks that Savannah's Historical Society designated 1,100 private buildings as worthy of restoration, and raised the money to renovate 900 of them. It occurs to me that this is the kind of medium-startling fact that anybody could make up, but that I am maximum-unlikely to check on. I accept it, and join the chorus of amazed noises. As we round a cobbled corner we come upon a smaller house that has been gutted for restoration. This one fronts right onto the sidewalk, so I limp up the single step for a look inside.

It is an open rectangle of rough bare brick — whatever plaster there once was has been entirely stripped — about twenty by thirty, the far wall divided in uneven thirds by the shells of two fireplaces. The thick beams are exposed some twenty feet overhead; the floor and floor joists have been removed so that the littered ground is three feet below the threshold, and there are deep slots in the brick that once held the massive joists. Excitement, mild but sudden, familiar, rises in me. Blond-bearded Toby from Philadelphia is beside me, also peering over the threshold.

"They'll plaster the brick," I say, "but they shouldn't."

"No," he agrees. "They should paint it and leave it bare. Insulate and leave the floor as low as possible."

"And no interior walls except for a bathroom. A loft at the far end."

"You wouldn't want to use both fireplaces at once, though. Turn one into a bookcase?"

"Or a kitchen flue."

Fairbanks David has rationalized himself into taking the Scottsville sign; we hoot at him because the sheriff's truck is whizzing by. We turn from the doorframe, and all of us head on toward the Hilton.

But while I walk, wobbling on the paving stones and sniffing pulp brine (and afterward, I'm afraid, well into the afternoon reading), I find myself thinking about this inane conversation, this minor kinship. I think about loving empty houses.

I must, over the course of a lifetime, have inspected several hundred untenanted dorm rooms, apartments, flats, and houses. The process has sometimes been discouraging, but never boring. I have twice in a foreign city pretended to be a prospective buyer in order to purchase a peek at what's available. Not that I'm an enthusiastic tourist of stately homes and renovated castles. No, what I like is not a sense of the sumptuous past but a promise of the possible future. I like picturing my books on the shelves and my treadle machine in the corner. I want the houses *empty*. I have never bought a house that had furniture in it, let alone inhabitants, and I have never resisted the impulse in even the most impossible awkwardness of space and ugly carpets to imagine what I could do with a bucket of paint and five hundred dollars. It would seem that I am not alone. Neither Toby from Philadelphia nor

I from Tallahassee has any intention, ever, of buying a house in Savannah, Georgia. And neither of us has to explain to the other that we have no such intention (nor, luckily, to the Savannah Historical Society, which would no doubt take a dim view of our anachronisms). The impulse to design, to plan, perhaps to interfere, is axiomatic with us both.

I'm reminded of an afternoon in the White Sands desert of New Mexico, where I had gone to visit a college friend. Her brother worked at the Proving Grounds (later called the Missile Range), and we had been given permission to wander in a stretch of untouristed dune. The whiteness of the sands was stunning, the sky so hot as to be white-blue itself. There were a few bleached stalks of grass here and there, a few chameleons with no reason to be anything but white, and mile upon mile of perfect sand undulating and shimmering in the heat. All afternoon we would park the car, race into that serene surface, destroy it with our footprints, and dive back into the car. We would drive until our previous path was out of sight and the horizon untrammeled perfection, and then we would get out and trammel it. We exhausted ourselves. We sweated. The sun went down and the desert began to chill. What were we up to? Still, the sight of unbroken undulating drifted pale sugar-fine sand was irresistible, and we ran into it again and left our mark.

Leaving our mark, I suppose, was the point. "The first impulse toward any art," says Robert Haas, "is to act on the world." And I have no doubt that all human beings share at least that much of the impulse toward art. We act on the world by setting our footprints on the shore, knowing that the sea will efface any sign of our having passed there. We make angels in the snow knowing they will melt. When the azaleas are at their fullest we *must* bring them inside and improve on the density and symmetry of their arrangement, knowing they will die faster indoors, knowing that the bushes are indifferent to our vandalism. Some people must carve their initials on the biggest tree and some must plant flags on the moon. I must buy fabrics, and am so drawn to the length and drape of silks, linens, woolens, to the nubs and slicks of texture, that they mount uncut in the cupboard; and then I must cut into them and sew them up, knowing perfectly well that I will never have as much pleasure of the clothes I make as I have of the yardage on the shelves. Just this moment I have rolled a sheet of fresh bond in my typewriter — which for all I know came out of the smelly mills of Savannah — with the minute familiar pleasure that attaches itself to a blank sheet, knowing that within half an hour I will have spoiled its whiteness with ill-typings, x'ed-out phrases, and imperfect word choice, so that the clear idea in my mind will be muddled and muddied. Yet I will do it. Try and stop me!

At some point in the seventeenth century Ben Jonson took a quill and a sheet of fresh paper or parchment and wrote:

> Have you seen but a bright lily grow
> Before rude hands have toucht it?
> Have you markt but the fall of the snow
> Before the soil hath smutcht it?

The poem is a series of conventional images in praise of a beautiful virgin, but by the end of the poem she has been not only admired but felt, smelled, and tasted; she has been toucht and smutcht. The very thing that makes her valuable makes her violable. Ben Jonson understood the impulse well.

And yet, for the most part our impulse to imprint ourselves on the world is not a rape of the world. Putting footprints in the sand is not the same thing as assaulting beaches. The need of the mind's eye to people an empty house with people, furnish it with furniture, is not invasion either. Controlling the parts in a sentence is not the same thing as controlling lives. It is true that no beaver gnaws and no ant tunnels unless it intends to live in what it has made, and that makes the beaver and the ant superior to us in our consumption. But the human mind is a piece of the natural world as well, and the nature of the human mind is to imprint itself. Even if to some extent we mangle what we touch, even if every walk on the beach is a sort of hobble, that is who we are, acting on the world with a futile cry of *Me!* against the sands, the snows, the empty spaces.

Eleventh Hour

lex and I had been in England for the fall semester, and we'd decided that he would stay in school there when I came back to Florida.

Born in Sussex, transplanted to America at the age of five, my younger son had steadfastly refused to root. He'd insisted on his British citizenship; he was *English*, later *Arthurian*, eventually *Punk*. Now his whole seventeen-year-old will was engaged in staying in London: his grades had dramatically improved; his energy was high; his teachers said to go on, he'd be fine; the director of the Florida State London Program had found him a place in the dorm, where he'd have friends and at least the illusion of oversight. I know the difference between an umbilical cord and an apron string, and on the whole I'm pretty good at letting go. I could put two thousand miles between us with no more link than a telephone line. What I could not do was abandon him at the holiday, and so I had shipped his brother via MasterCard to join us for a couple of weeks.

I'm a fool about Christmas, and the tradition is that I start in October assuring the boys that this year it's going to be minimal. I really mean it: there will be a modest, a sensible, a positively penurious exchange of presents. I give them good reasons. They solemnly understand, soon begin to snigger, and thereafter affect to tolerate my lapses into the baking of pies, works of wrapping-paper art, humming of carols, and decking of the halls. By the time I have staggered into debt again to give them this year's heart's desire, I have also erected an elaborate deception by the rules of which neither may know of the other's major gifts, because each would then detect that I had evened things out with similar extravagance.

But this year I did mean it, on the grounds that Tim's trip to England was more than I could afford and by far the most expensive thing

he wanted. We would have mere trinkets to exchange, and our celebration would consist of going to a Restoration comedy on Christmas
Eve afternoon, and then to dinner at the historic Café Royal with our
wonderful friends the Thaddeuses (or Thaddei), who also happened to
be in England for the holiday.

Now, my sons are so unlike each other that it is not possible they
were produced from the same two sets of chromosomes, which they
were, nor that they were raised under the same single-parent effort of
Spock and spaghetti, which they were. All parents say that, more or
less, but in my case it's really true. No, it *really* is. Tim is Episcopalian,
Republican, impeccable, and polite. Alex is a radical left-wing feminist anarchist. At the moment they were both quasi-bald — Tim buzz-
cut for ROTC and Alex mohawked for busking around Piccadilly
Circus, where American tourists sometimes slipped him a pound note
to take his picture (he'd been away from Florida ten weeks) — and
they would have looked quite a lot alike if Tim were not wearing an
Alligator shirt with his Jaeger blazer and Top-Siders while Alex had
ripped one sleeve out of the famous Dead Bird T-shirt and strapped a
cricket guard over one leg of his shredded jeans. Tim, who thinks all
anti-capitalists should be shipped to the colonies, is personally a
peacemaker, easygoing as a housemate, and empathetic in a crisis.
Alex, who espouses universal brotherhood and boasts that he's a
wimp, stirs emotional turmoil and wreaks havoc in any room big
enough to hold two people and a boom box.

So it was no great surprise when Alex declined the culture. But
he said that, yeah, okay, he could handle wearing a tie if it meant snails
and trifles at a hotshot Victorian restaurant. Tim offered him the loan
of an elegant double-breasted suit. Alex declined again. He would wear
his Salvation Army polyester, which had a certain street-smart *je ne
sais quoi*.

Meanwhile the tradition unfolded: lapses into tinsel furbishing on
my part, the affectation of tolerance on theirs. The boys had twenty
pounds each to spend on me, ten of their own and ten from my father,
whose gifts they were to choose for me. Tim began bringing home
packages and declaring this and that corner of our tiny flat off limits.
Alex was as usual leaving it to the eleventh hour. I garnered a pile of
appropriately British kilt pins, records, T-shirts, and Shetland sweaters. On the twenty-third Tim belied his nonchalance by coming home

with the six-foot tree, whereupon I ran out for lights and ornaments, rolled out a pie crust, and dashed out Christmas Eve morning to decorate my credit card once more, with the Bogart trench coat Tim coveted and the million-decibel amplifier that Alex could not do without and that I would not, after all, be around to listen to. I stashed one of these in an empty suitcase and covered the other with the dirty laundry, piled the wrapped packages under the tree — I don't defend it, brassy American conspicuous consumption by anybody's standards — and I was ready.

But it was an oddly nervous day. Alex had moved into the dorm, and he failed to come by for his lengthened trousers before Tim and I left for the theatre. I didn't know if he had his key, or if he would think to check with the doorman for the one I had left him. All through *The School for Scandal* I was distracted with the knowledge that this might be our last Christmas together for many years, and the apprehension that something was going wrong. Among the gilt hangings of the Café Royal Tim and I greeted the Thaddei — literary Jan, nuclear physicist Patrick, and their two Harvard-bound, articulate, opera-loving, poised and perfect teenagers, Eva and Michael — and unfolded our square-yard linen napkins. Alex wasn't there. I slipped back out to check the street, toward Piccadilly Circus where the punks were playing, toward Oxford Circus where the last-minute shoppers hoisted their burdens and jousted for cabs. I went back in, made some bright remark at his expense, made light of it, and ordered my hors d'oeuvre. I engaged young Michael on the subject of *Lord of the Flies*. But the glitter was off the glassware, my stomach sour. Was Alex actually willing to stand us up on Christmas Eve?

Half an hour later he sailed in, dashing in his brother's two-piece suit and polished shoes, debonair with his apologies — so sorry to keep us waiting, he'd thought we said 7:30—and energized with Christmas mischief.

"All your presents are wrapped and under the tree, Mum. I gotcha nothing but toys. I decided you were old enough to get toys for Christmas. Tim! Don't you think it's time the Mum got toys for Christmas?" For the next hour and a half he scattered charm, and I tucked into roast duck. We displayed the tradition for our laughing friends: me faking a holdout for Christmas morning while the boys used logic, nonsense, and blatant appeals to mother-love to convince me we should go straight home and open the presents.

Which of course we did. We took a taxi up Regent Street under the arch of shining angels, then sat with more coffee and chocolate mints, shredding paper on the floor and tossing ribbons in that heightened sense of family in a foreign setting.

Tim had chosen my gifts with characteristic and slightly somber thoughtfulness: an Indian silk scarf, a pin of carved teak, a simple wrap-around skirt. Alex had got me the aforesaid nothing-but-toys. The first was a Matchbox car, a sleek little Mercedes — no use to me, but indicating a certain flattery of my style. The second was a teddy bear about four inches high, with pink plastic earrings. Well, all right, rather sweet. Giving his childhood back, maybe, for me to take home with me?

It was very nearly midnight by the time he brought out the third and last of his gifts. This one appeared, from its shape and size, to be another Matchbox car — but then I have taught them to be expert at disguises. I took off the wrapping to reveal the box and waited to get the joke. It was another Matchbox car. The picture showed a garish miniature transport truck, and when I opened the box the yellow snout of this truck rolled forward onto the flap.

Alex was sitting upright on the couch, grinning prodigiously, and my roast duck and trifle took a slow turn in my belly. I looked back at the truck. Alex knew, and knew I knew, that two Matchbox cars and a miniature teddy bear had not cost twenty pounds. Five, maybe, which meant that he had pocketed fifteen pounds. His excitement was a ruse to cover the fact that he had stolen the Christmas money, part of what I had given him, all of my father's. And it was a challenge, too. In the time it would take to tip the truck out of the box I had to decide whether I would confront him and ruin Christmas for all of us — how many years before we'd have another together, to make repairs? — or keep the betrayal to myself, save Tim's present pleasure and Alex's face. He knew I had to make a choice. It was a test of the grimmest sort a child could offer.

Sick, I tipped the ugly little truck into my hand. Its wheels rolled across my palm, which was already sweating. I would have to face him. And I would have to back it up by returning the amplifier. Otherwise I would signal that he was not responsible, a child still, under mom's protection, and I would not be able to leave him behind. But it was hard, the rupture of so much ancient innocence, so much family equivalent of Santa Claus. The box rocked heavily in my fingers, tipped back once and forward once.

And out tumbled onto the back of the truck a minute mouse, no bigger than my thumbnail, of hand-carved Austrian crystal with jet eyes and a sterling spring for a tail. It was silly and beautiful, a diamond whimsy, and I sat staring at it remembering seeing such things in the windows of the jewelers on Bond Street, while it dawned on me how many hoardings of lunch money it represented beyond what Alex had to spend. I cried, of course, not because a crystal mouse was exactly what I always wanted, but because out of my fear I had been asking the wrong questions and getting the wrong answers. What other kind of lying have I taught them, these grown boys, but to put rings in shoe boxes and amplifiers in the dirty clothes at Christmas?

"I thought you stole the money!" I wailed, being of a confessional nature myself, to the great satisfaction of both boys.

I am in the process of wrapping presents again, to ship to London. Alex wants a phase shifter for his guitar, and I don't know what that is, but I've ordered one from The Music Box on Charing Cross Road. The mouse sits next to my mother's wedding photo on my windowsill, perfectly useless — a toy, see — except that when I put the tip of my finger to the tip of its coiled tail, the tail springs free with a *Boing!* — reminding me not to mistrust the kids one minute earlier than the last minute of the eleventh hour.

Dad Scattered

The corpse was nobody I knew. I'm told this is a common feeling. It was skinny, which he never was, and his remaining flesh had thinned and contracted so that although it ought to have been rucked about his jaw it was not; it was taut, like paper wet-shrunk over the balsa bones of a model plane. They had unaccountably repeated that his "color was good" — Gladys who watched him dwindle, the oncologist who pronounced him untreatable, the girl aide who folded his stiff legs in her golden arm to lever him into the wheelchair while the cells ate themselves from the lymph nodes outward, through the roof of his mouth, all down the marrow, while the white corpuscles multiplied amuck to burn his heart with the final indigestion. Even Aunt Jessie, sister as heroine, saying, "Don't wait too long, it won't be long," added, "His color is still good."

All the same, now he was gray. The half-moons of his fingernails were slate. I, yes, turned down the cover to see his hands. He was still warm. I hadn't missed his death by more than half an hour. I lay my cheek against his forehead and felt nothing. I forgot that one feels nothing and I felt: nothing, nothing. I thought coolly: everyone goes through this, sooner or later, more or less. A keening sound came from me — false, effective. I recognized it as an appropriate sound.

You will think I mean that I felt numb, but I did not. Numb is a feeling. I felt the paper warmth. The hard proximity of his skull beneath it. I murmured some words that I knew to be false but that would have been the true words I would have murmured had I not been false. Aunt Jessie was there. It later occurred to me that he was there.

Now for the moment it has come down to this: a brown carton smaller than a whiskey carton, on the deep mint plush between Bud and me.

"I *hate* that carpet," Gladys said viciously before she went to bed. "It shows every footprint!" Dad has been dead a month, but his ashes have not yet been received by the Neptune Society in California. I look for his footprints in the carpet pile even though I vacuumed this morning. I have been in Phoenix since Thursday and have emptied the closet, trashed the ancient toiletries, boxed the clothes for Goodwill, sorted papers into *garbage, important*, and *curiosity*. Jenny will get the woodworking tools; the machine tools will be sold. Tim will have the tartan scarf and Alex the Dior robe. Gladys will get the stocks, the canoe will go to the Boy Scouts, and I have gathered into this carton what I think Bud and I should look over together. Bud arrived at noon and already the three of us, Gladys and he and I, have settled the formalities of the small inheritance. Since the will was declared void, we agreed on splitting it three equal ways. The lawyer remarked on our amiability. "I've known — literally — families that fought over a toothbrush." Now Gladys, unamiable, has gone to bed, and Bud and I are here assembled to see if a toothbrush will emerge.

"This stopwatch," I begin arbitrarily. "I can't figure out where it came from. I never saw it; I don't know if it was his or not."

I begin arbitrarily. I use the term "now" loosely, and variously. I choose this point on the green plush as "now" but might choose any other because tense itself is a fiction. Really, everything is past. At Christmas Gladys will say, "I keep thinking he's in the bedroom, or he's run down to the store. Is that crazy?" Over a course of months I will still be expecting him to die. An airport pager calling for some other Janet, the phone ringing at any slightly out-of-the-ordinary hour, myself surfacing from a dream at dawn — there will be that minute clench in the stomach that represents a readying for the blow. Then immediately I will remember that there's nothing left to fear. The awful is already over. In February I will see, in London, a Morgan roadster, and develop the full intention of asking Dad what he thinks of the Morgan as a car.

However, for the moment, it has come down to this: a box of bric-a-brac, a life's debris, the watch that may or may not have been his and will now become the property of this or that other. What is surprising about his belongings is that there are so few of them. He lived for invention, making, tools, construction. He loved manufacture, advertising, a gimmick, a thingamabob. He doted on rivets, rubber, templates, glue. He was the only man I ever knew excited by the doohickeys of daily maintenance: oil change, furnace filters, rust removers, saddle soap. If that is who he was, why didn't he invest in more Turtle Wax, more toggle bolts and caulk guns we could claim for our inheritance?

In fact there are five pocket watches, which suggests some relationship to time of which we ought to know the significance: that he was especially prompt, aware of history, afraid of old age, cautious, driven. More likely it represents a love of gadgets. Five watches, two antiques that might have belonged to Grandpa Lawrence or Uncle Art, one stopwatch of some cheap, weightless, miracle metal, one never-used Westclox still in its box; and — the only one I care about — a silver disc so flat that it reminds me of the dollar pancakes mom used to flip on the griddle.

However, that is also the only watch Bud wants. He wants to buy a silver chain for it and take it home to his wife, Michelle. And, after all, the two antiques will go to my progeny, who are boys.

"Remember that old pancake griddle we used to have?"

"Yes, why?"

"I wonder what happened to it."

We sit on the mint green floor, Bud cross-legged and me with my legs crooked to one side, although I am fifty and he is fifty-four and we don't often sit this way anymore. It has something to do with being siblings, children. It has something to do with being orphans. He is bald and black-bearded; he used to amuse my boys and his girls by saying that his hair had melted and slid down his chin. He is loose and lean in the shoulders and thickening at the waist, heading for pear-shaped, like Dad.

But Bud was four when I was born, and so I see all his ages layered in him, and of these the thickening middle-aged man before me is the least real. He is still, as I am to myself, a child to me. I see him barely teenage, forelock dipped over his eye in a black curl, a yellow pencil stub behind his ear, cool nerd, already sardonic, the journalist. Whereas Dad, being grown when I came into the world, is in my memory a single and continuous self.

Our father's body was soft and loose; his upper arms jiggled when he ran. In summer in the swimming pools he wore blue twill boxer trunks with the string hanging out. He hitched the suit up over his girth. He had saggy breasts and a loose, broad belly that hung forward to hold up his trunks. He was not much concerned with fat but didn't like to be chided for it. There was dark hair neither thick nor sparse over his chest and down his arms. I found this apparition mildly, but only mildly, embarrassing, because it meant old man, a person of father-age. My father's body was never otherwise, was never trim or muscular or more or less wrinkled than I remember it at the pools — vast and crowded Encanto, or intimate and shabby Monte Vista, or Martinez's south of town, where a real stream, cold from underground, ran through a wire fence and into the slimy slanted side of the pool. That place was always full of a nervous mix of skin colors, these being also present in my mother's voice in the words "South Central." There Dad and I stood under a waterfall and froze to the bone, the purpose being then to fling ourselves back out on the bank in the baking sun. And these swimming sessions continued, did they not, into my teen years, into my adulthood whenever I came home? They seem to belong to the easy swing of childhood, but I remember, once, driving south on Central, telling Dad about being hopelessly in love with an unavailable man, so surely they never really stopped? There was, perhaps, a period after I was eleven that they stopped?

"Look at these."

There are bundles of pencils, charcoal, Eagle, Eberhardt, Castell, bound in rubber bands like firewood faggots. There are boxes of new Pink Pearl erasers, his supply of which he never let dwindle. There are templates in translucent green, translucent amber, silver metal; a series of neon orange triangles, two sets of German drafting tools in their velvet-lined boxes, which we remember precisely because they were kept so carefully locked away. There's also a single French curve of clouded plastic — called French but suggesting something more exotic, Oriental, a peacock or paisley, and representing every possible shape, proportion, and variation on the curve known to architecture. Neither Bud nor I can use this mysterious tool, but both of us want it and are hesitant to say so. It falls to me for no better reason than that it comes after the watch, and Bud commandeered the watch.

These were the tools and whatsits of his trades. He was a plasterer first, before either of us was born, then a machinist, a brick mason, carpenter, contractor, a tool and die maker, a home designer, an architect without a license. During World War II he put airplane wings together, and in the age of missiles he polished missile parts. He invented a spacer for glass bricks, a house number that attracted and refracted light, a toy propeller, a parking tower for trailers so that low-income transients with a taste for culture like himself would have cheap access to a city. He liked signs and advertising. He kept an ear out for slogans, jingles. He took an interest in the atom.

"Remember this?"

It's an address book, or rather not a book at all but a hinged flat metal box with an arrow that zips down the alphabet printed on the side. You set the arrow and push a lever; the top flips up to reveal . . . now, at the letter *C*, the words *cupboard, closet, circuit, counter, cost, construction, ceiling*, and, set apart below, *kitchen* with the *k* double-underlined, in case he looked for it on the wrong page.

He was dyslexic, though none of us heard that term until his middle age, and it was not applied to him till he was in his seventies. Up to then he just was a rotten speller. He could draft a house design to scale with an eye so true it hardly needed a ruler to it, but he spelled *linen* with two *n*'s and *closet* with an *it*. Mom made him the spelling kit of the words he needed, the one-syllable pitfalls: *den, porch, sill*; and the confounding illogical English multisyllabism: *masonite, bathtub, piping, quarter-inch, foundation*.

"Do you want it?"

"What would I do with it? But otherwise . . . well, okay, yes."

There are paperclips and spring clips, staples, connectors of every sort, but nothing to connect. A paper punch and boxes of little reinforcement rings. There are a half-dozen blotters, blue ink-sopped on the back and on the front a miniature calendar of the month, the name of Del Webb Supply, and a picture of a golden babe, this one in a red velvet skating rig, that one in wisps of blue sunsuit, another as a waitress in roller skates. All their skirts skim rounded buns, the cheeks like peaches. All their breasts are globes with buttons. What is to be done with them? There was so little prurience in him that to have had three Petti calendars in his drawer was proof of — what? That he was in the building trade.

There are tie tacks in the form of airplanes studded with semi-precious stones, initialed cufflinks, mother-of pearl collar studs, and a bolo tie with a kachina slide. Dad liked to think of himself as dapper, and in later years he came to adorning himself with decorator colors. When he was no longer building he would wear maroon jackets and morning glory ties, lime polyester trousers with lemon shirts, baby blue Monkey Ward tattersall with ultramarine cuffed duck, pink shirts with painted ties. His color was still good.

There are coins in jars and purses, pennies in scrubbed-out shoe polish tins, nickels in mint boxes, a whole former mayonnaise pint in quarters. He always checked the edge of dimes and quarters for a copper strip. He had a collection of several hundred dollars' worth that were pure silver. But that he sold, for silver weight, at the handsome profit of six hundred dollars, which he then invested in a Broadway show that flopped. These coins are ordinary chicken feed, the silver layered with copper, and not enough to seem worthwhile, qua change.

After mom died, there was a period when Dad called me late at night. "Can anyone be listening to this?" he'd say. "Is it possible your phone is tapped?"

"Dad, why would anyone tap my phone?"

"Don't tell anybody. Buy silver."

"What?"

"Are you putting your money into silver bars?"

"Dad, I'm putting my money into corn flakes. I don't have any to invest."

"Set some aside. Buy silver."

"Why?"

"America is going to have a depression; it's going to make the thirties look like a piece of cake."

This went on maybe twice a week for a couple of months and then it stopped. When I told Marjie about it, she said, "Oh! See? He can't allow himself to have depression; no one of that generation can. So America's going to have it for him."

My reaction to this was relief and gratitude. It made sense to me. It made metaphoric sense; it was not craziness, it was a coping mechanism. Anyone can tell you: even nuts is functional if it's a coping mechanism.

There's a coping saw. A hacksaw, four packets of new blades. Why is this what's left us? A set of spark plugs. A distributor cap. An automotive coil of some sort neither of us recognizes.

"No," Bud says. "It's for a boat, part of an outboard. I don't know how I know."

We lived in the desert, but Bud and I both remember Dad best at water's edge. We remember him launching a sailboat, dragging a canoe off the stony beach, always in some version or other of the twill trunks over which his belly hung in a pale parabola.

We went to Balboa and Laguna and rented sailboats for more per hour than he made per hour. We went to Banff and took pictures of ourselves in a canoe against the glaciers and the glacial sky. We rode a speedboat over the surf from Catalina, bucking waves as hard as boards. Dad built a motorboat, and we took it to Lake Apache where we caught one after another of luminous yellow perch just barely big enough to eat. We took a trailer to Seal Beach and set it up beside the channel, where Dad worked through the summer, designing houses on a board set aslant over the tiny sink while Bud and I stabbed crabs on the channel rocks with a nail on the end pole and walked under the highway in a tunnel riven by a trickle of dirty water.

Dad went to Alaska after we were too old to vacation with him and Mom any more, and there invented his famous (to us) and still-feasible (why not?) "Car-go Boat," an aluminum flat barge so light it could be pulled by a Volkswagen Bug, and powered by the axle of the car once you got to water and drove aboard her.

When he died the garage was full of canoe, long plastic tubes he was gluing or laminating to the sides in a mistaken, we believe, belief that he could make the airflow lift the boat above the water's friction. The boat was ruined, but the Boy Scouts took it anyway.

And he who so loved the ocean is now to go into it. The Neptune Society will drop his ashes off a sailboat between Long Beach and Catalina. Except that they have apparently mislaid the ashes.

Our father's body is in transit from A. L. Moore and Sons of Phoenix to the Neptune Society in Los Angeles, who will scatter him into the sea where he most often chose to be when he had a choice. We didn't have him embalmed, and the casket that went for cremation was some kind of composition essentially cardboard. It was what he wanted, cremation and least fuss. We did not dispatch our father's body in a cardboard box in order to save money, though of course there is a residual guilt, as if we had. In those days after his death I thought involuntarily and often of cremation, and once I dreamed of it. I had heard somewhere that body fat rises to the surface. When I dreamed his burning, I saw his body as it used to be, not the paper husk of him that died but the soft swimmer, the fleshy pear. I saw him blister.

We sent him to the fire in a cardboard box, and here we have what's left in a cardboard box. There are jars of keys. We spill them on the rug. Skeleton keys and house keys, car keys from makes of car we know he owned and from makes we know he didn't. Suitcase and briefcase keys, though he never had a briefcase; old and gold, tiny and light keys, a pair that are etched with filigree, a dozen Master Lock, padlock, and locker keys. Keys to nothing. There are a few we have dealt with before, deposit box keys that we thought would solve the riddle of the garbled will, so baffling in its combination of legalese and faulty grammar, clearly specifying what to do if this or that beneficiary predeceased another, but not specifying what went to whom if Bud and Gladys and I were all, as we are, living. But there was no deposit box and these were keys to nothing.

There is a wide translucent loop of red celluloid, scored around its circumference about three-quarters of the way across. We both recognize it at the same moment: it's a band from the Dictaphone that dad had when we were — what? — in fourth and eighth grades, and he had decided to write essays on topics humorous and scientific. If we could find a Dictaphone circa 1945, we could hear his voice; we could learn at least what he had wanted, then, to be heard, when later he wanted so little, and then nothing, to escape his mouth.

When I was five and six I sat in his lap facing the radio as if it were a fire; and he told of his youth, how he learned to drive a motorcar from a book because he was not allowed to touch the wheel, how he became mechanic to the Boy Scouts and got to travel free, to Louisiana, Saulte Sainte Marie, Yellowstone. My dad could remember what went wrong with each of those Boy Scout touring cars, the mis-wiring of the Model T in 1922, the radiator leak in the 1929 Pierce Arrow. He could talk a blue streak, he could get on a jag and go with it, the way a distributor distributes, the plot of a movie, a new plastering swirl technique, the chronology of a trip and what he saw on it, stalactites, the mother bear, the mud geyser, the redwood with a girth of ninety feet. One night Bud asked him about the cars he'd owned, and Dad went through all forty-five in order, the dates he bought them, the year, model, and condition of each, the price he paid and the price he got when he moved onto the next.

He loved the theater, radio, the movies, Charles Wesley's hymns, Ken Murray's Blackouts, Ziegfield's Follies, *My Friend Irma, My Friend Flicka*. He liked to be read to, he liked to hear "pieces," he took us to Hollywood to stand in line for free tickets to *Stella Dallas*. He wanted stories, skits, elocution, anecdotes, the news, a shaggy dog.

But after mom died he quieted, and over the eleven years with Gladys he spoke less and less. When cancer took him, the voice went first. In the hospital he scarcely spoke at all. *Yes, no. I guess so. So you say.* I wanted to shout at him, shake him. "Don't you realize this is our last chance?" But I didn't need anyone to tell me that it was his death and he was allowed to conduct it as he chose.

I flew back and forth to Arizona six times for his death. On the penultimate trip I asked if he got discouraged, and he answered that.

"Oh, yes, I lie here at night. If I had a way to kill myself I would."

He said this with an inflection that made it clear he expected me to be shocked. When I said, "I know," he picked up his head from the pillow an inch or so. "If I could get some of that stuff. I can't remember the name."

I knew what he meant. One of his old stories, a favorite, was about the time in Bowie in the early thirties, when he was working in the grocery store, that he sold a drinking glass to a man who drank poison from it that night in his hotel room.

"Cyanide," I said.

"Yes. If I knew how to get some of that . . ."

It was a question, a request. I sat thinking of the consummate innocence of a man who, in 1987, would think of cyanide; the implied content of a man who hadn't followed the fashions in suicide for sixty years.

"I'm sorry you have to go through that sort of discouragement, Dad," I said. He took this for the refusal that it was, and retreated into silence.

Later I told Marjie the curious circumstance of Dad's lymphoma, that it manifested into the roof of his mouth although there are no lymph nodes in the mouth. Marjie said, "Oh, my God. Of course." She meant that he would not open his mouth to let the poison out.

Three years from now I will read that it is a peculiar, modern form of self-righteousness to blame the cancerous for their cancers in this way.

"What's this?"

Here is *Machinery's Handbook*, eleventh edition, 1942, published by the Industrial Press and according to the title page distributed in Britain from a wartime address of 17 Marine Parade, Brighton. The machinists' tools have gone to auction, their sleek oak box is on its way to my home to hold jewelry on the green felt floors of its long flat drawers; but I did not know what to do with the book, covered in malleable leather, three inches thick, and indexed with black and gilt tabs like that other bible. I open it at random, show Bud a table of "Feeds for Box Tools," divided into *roughing* and *finishing* from one-sixteenth to five-eighths *diameter of stock*, and specifying the *brass rod, machine steel*, and *tool steel feed per revolution*. The table is precise to within thousandths of an inch. What it means to me is: nothing. I know roughly what *rough* and *finish* mean. I have generic concepts for *feed, box*, and *steel*. Here is exactitude, its clues and symbols, and I am illiterate. What shall we do with it? It is out of date; no one who would understand it would now find it useful. I will take it home, I will put it back in the center slot of the tool box whence it came, among the alien imprecision of earrings and African beads.

I'm illiterate in so many signs. There's so much that I can't operate or read, memories that don't explain or fit, that make no more useful legacy than another thingamabob in the cardboard box.

This one, for instance, a memory slightly distorted, as the memory of a place is distorted by the photographs that remain of having visited it: I think this took place when I was in sixth grade, my eleventh year. What I now recall is that Mom was dressing for a PTA meeting, putting on her powder and running a comb through her hair, and I lay down on the double bed to chat to her while she dressed. Dad came in and lay down beside me, we all talked, and then she left. He began to tell me a story — memory makes it the one about the log that they tied on the back of the Ford with the shot brakes to drive it down the mountain at Yellowstone. I don't know if this is right. What is clear in my mind is that I was getting sleepy, and that he reached across with his right hand and put it on my nub of left breast, began to squeeze, a little half-laugh in his throat as he carried on with the story, my skin working in his fist. What I remember best is the stinging of my ears, my heart crashing under his hand, part fear, part disbelief. I remember that what I thought came hammering clear and slow: *This has never happened before. No father has ever done this. This is the worst thing that has ever happened in the world.*

Later Marjie will ask me to draw the scene, and when I do, it will be the view from over my left shoulder, looking down onto the bed, the two heads, two bodies, four legs, his hand across my body. "Funny," I'll say, "I've drawn myself without arms or a mouth."

"Of course. How would you defend yourself?"

And this seems right to me, revelatory, neat as a pin.

I don't remember what I did. Memory is numb, as that breast has been without feeling forty years. It never happened again. I remember that afterward I nursed this terrible secret with great self-pity and a sense of apocalypse; that the daily events of home took on again the same pattern of familiar dullness but would suddenly reverse and reveal themselves to me as a terrible lie. I remember that I pitied and disdained my mother, and also that most of the time I forgot about it. I remember that in college I looked back, wise and cool, thinking: *well, they've always told me I was given to melodrama.* I remember thinking both that it was the end of the world and that I had made too much of it in my mind. I don't remember when I first heard of incest or abuse as a possible human phenomenon. I don't remember when I learned how much worse it could be, or how apocalyptic it always was. It was not a major subject then, as it became. It didn't seem to anyone to explain a life.

Now Bud and I sit surrounded with the debris, and it has to remind us both of Christmas, the gifts denuded of their wrappings and diminished into little piles.

"No toothbrush," Bud says. "Our dad raised good-natured kids."

I agree. Darwin said that animals make noise in order to augment whatever feeling is necessary at the time. A dog growls to make itself ferocious, and a cat hisses to be dangerous. Soldiers joke going into battle because pretending to feel brave can make you brave. Now Bud and I praise each other, how generous we have been to each other over our father's death. It makes us helpful to say we are so. It makes us love each other more to say we do.

Marjie will say, "Why can't you get angry? Really you are, deeply, angry!"

And maybe she's right. But it doesn't feel like something too deep to feel. It seems to me that what I think is also what I feel: that this was a man so innocent it never crossed his mind — no, rather, that he felt some guilt but was able in the moment's impulse to rationalize it, and that later he put it out of mind.

"No man can do that! He knew what he was doing!"

No doubt she's right. I can't be so innocent as to believe he was innocent, can I?

But it continues stubbornly to seem that he did something awful not meaning to, and forgot it after. There's so much evidence around. There's so much stuff here, keys to nothing, staples, paper clips.

My friend Mose will tell me, oh, a matter of years from now, about the moment of death of his cat Max. At the moment of death, he will say, Max seemed to shrink; there was a sudden, subtle diminishing. And Mose could see how the notion came about, of the spirit leaving the body. He could see that something seemed to disperse itself invisibly into space. Then I will think of Dad, the skin shrunk over his bones, how I felt nothing, and also felt that it was not he; how he was dispersed into memory, past knowing, beyond judgment.

Here's another tie tack, this one in the form of a turbine engine.

A spring weight with a hook.

Foreign coins, from countries he never visited: Italy, France, a set of six Imperial dollars intended for the occupation of America by Japan. An English sixpence, from the one "foreign" country he did get to. In a hardwood frame, a collection of Republican campaign buttons mounted on red felt. I like Ike. Win with Nixon. Elect Dewey. Among seven children and grandchildren he could claim one Republican. What will we do with these?

Bud calls the Neptune Society, but the ashes have not arrived.

Hair

was maybe thirty-five, six. I lay in a high bed between enameled walls for one of those operations that needn't be named because it's unspellable. The black nurse arrived with basin, towel, soap, razor and ready cheer. I moaned, and the muscles of my stomach clenched, maybe with fear, maybe with more minor dreads, remembering the shaving of my pubes when my first son was born, my angry suspicion that it was unnecessary — and the long scratchiness of the hair growing out.

Now the buoyant nurse told me to turn on my side and raise a knee. Oh, I said, relieved, she wasn't going to shave me then?

"Just in back! Oh, lord, love, I'm not going to take your glory!"

She drew the vowel out, voluptuous. I sighed with relief and pride. My glooory. It was so. The hair on my head is fine and straight, the stuff I shave under arms, on shins, is negligible and spiky. But there! Then! A nether Afro, black with red highlights, luxuriant, an ebullient mass. Brushed, it would spring back instantly into ringlets. The American euphemism "beaver" is ignorant, a thick flat metaphor, nothing like. But a "bush," yes, resilient, silky, and sunny; it was a ready growth, warm May sprout, moss and glossy.

I remember the delicate baldness of girlhood, and how as a child I a little fearfully imagined myself in that goatee. Now, the other side of glory, I look at the thinness of my fur and find it somewhat stingy of nature, mean-natured, not necessary, that I have become thus sparse.

Nobody, I take it, minds but me. It is not a death, a serious separation, is not a grief. I seem to function better, come to that, than in the glory days. Hormones are keeping my bone marrow dense, knowing better how to choose a lover keeps me at better joy.

More. I'm lucky. By the time she was my age my grandmother wore on her head a half-wig called a "transformation"; by this age my mother's skull showed blue-white beneath the "poodle" cut crimped to hide it; in his forties my brother was egg-pated above his beard. I've escaped this Pierce-side-of-the family tendency to baldness, and my barber who styles himself a stylist tells me that there's no sign I'm thinning on top.

Only below, this bush of best youth, this kinky growth, this sable V, this little lawn, this springing grass, this private isle, reminds me that the very hairs are numbered.

What do you say to the losses of age? Oh, well. Oh, well.

Tone

K., who has a younger lover, moans that he's always wanting her on top. Why does she dislike this? I thought we fought through the fifties, the sixties, to gain the right to that position. I thought we wanted access to men who allowed, liked, preferred, requested it. I thought it was a distinct advantage of the younger lover, the liberated generation. I thought we fought to overturn "missionary" laws.

No. I know perfectly well what she means. She says, "Your face is so much better on your back."

This is not very articulate, but it brings that discovery back with a rush. I was doing something sweet. P. had no bedroom mirror and I had a spare. This one was big and clear and old, with a many-times white-painted frame of heavy Victorian gingerbread. The glass was loose in the frame and I was going to secure it before taking it to him for long-term loan — an indefinite, commitment sort of loan. I drove the little nails around the back of the frame, covered the join with heavy tape, then turned it over on the carpet to check the paint for nicks. Straddled hands and knees over the silvered glass, I caught sight of my face. Stopped shocked. I watched the crawling creature warily. Its skin and chin pulled forward off the bone, the jowls slid into the hollow of its cheeks. The bold eyes hid under the shelf of brow, which furrowed with the grainy pucker of the pull of center earth. The quality of the skin was that it foreshadowed its disintegration into cells of infinitesimal size. The opposite of taut is not, apparently, loose, but netlike. The wrinkles I am accustomed to seeing in my face are few and deep — laugh lines, crow's feet, furrows. These were hairline fissures dividing cell and cell.

This was not me. I know my bad side from my good, I know I am capable of posturing for the mirror, I know what I look like without makeup, I have even imagined my own skull. But this was not me, not me. I hung over gravity, I regarded myself gravely: I became grave.

Crepe is death's fabric.

All epidermis aspires to the condition of elbow.

Aging is nature's own *Verfremdungseffekt*.

Because the idea of "tone" is a metaphor from music, I have co-opted the word "semiquaver" to describe this quality of skin. Dutifully doing the morning exercises that keep my spine from hurting, legs straight over my torso I watch my knees fall toward me, microcosms of erosion, miniatures of buckling earth, tan temblors of the meaning of change. The flesh semiquavers on my knees. I have become rather fond of the sight.

I ran into a very young woman at the vet's. In other times I'd have called her a girl. Her legs were thin and without definition but with adequate fullness of lovely flesh. Her ankles ran straight from her calves into her sox and sneakers. Her skin was flawless Florida tan, butterscotch-pudding smooth. I admired this skin for several seconds before I realized that I did not envy and did not *want* it. I would call its texture callow. A lovely accident of flesh, and, lo, I'll choose my own.

You think I'm lying for rhetoric's sake, but don't underestimate the part of change that happens behind the skin. The beauty of bark, or woodgrain; the sound of "texture": text-sure. I finger my lover's elbows forgivingly. We embrace in the frame of gingerbread. I like his aging. I believe, know, that he likes my flesh buckling, semiquavering, text-sure. I like us liking our aging. We feel, to me, to have traded some quality of mere appearance for superior sight.

I climb on top.

Hill

Aunt J. J., 82, is touring Alaska once again with W., her companion of forty years. W. is the elder but will not say by how much. I keep their itinerary on my calendar because by the time I get back from England they will be packing for Switzerland, and we'll need to catch up. After Switzerland it's the Delta Gamma convention, and then the World Future Conference. They live, when they're at home, in the Ozarks of Branson, MO, and J. J. has lately taken to country western. W. keeps up a correspondence with some hundred and twenty people they've run into on their travels. Mornings they power walk, though they just call it walking. "It's lucky," W. says, "once you have the time, to have the health, the means, and the inclination still to travel."

Meanwhile I talk to my stepmother, G., also 82, in the nursing home in Arizona. First I call the nurse, who wheels G. to her own phone; then I call her phone, which the nurse puts in her hand. G. can walk, but won't; so the circulation has dwindled, and her legs are purple blue. Amputation has been mentioned, though not to her. As soon as she hears my voice she begins to cry. "I just don't know how to cope with these interviews anymore," she says.

"What interview is that, dear?"

"Oh, well, you know your dad is always being interviewed by these magazines, and you never know exactly how much you ought to tell them."

My dad died in 1987. So far as I know he was never interviewed by a magazine. G. straightens the sob out of her voice and sighs. "It seems like I just can't figure it all out. I don't know how to keep everything together."

She knows, and means, that her mind is going, almost gone — though she articulates very clearly what she wants. She wishes she could dig a long ditch and just lie down in it and not get up. She wishes an angel would come and lift her out of all this mess.

I ask stupidly if she got the book, the sweaters. Does she see the picture of me and P. on her dresser? Does she remember that we came out to visit her a few weeks ago?

"Couldn't you come over just for a few minutes now?"

"I'm in Florida, though. It's two thousand miles."

"Florida!" she says. "Florida!"

I dream that my grandmother — who had the white-curled, corsetted look of a Dick-and-Jane granny — has grown chic. Her hair is pulled back in a dark chignon, her face has narrowed toward a prow-like chin. She wears a sleek suit of gray flannel, ankles crossed above her pumps. She asks where I would like to go to dinner. The food in the Governor's Club where she lives is not bad, she says, but she thought I might like something more exotic.

I might like something more exotic. G. is in tears again, talking of the angel, whom I see with snow-white wings against a backdrop of Alaskan glacier. "All these people, it's not that they mistreat us" — she is sharp enough to give the staff its due. "But I can't do everything they want, gadding about all over the place. I can't. I wish that angel would come and wrap its wings around me, and just hold me until all this is over."

I share genes with Aunt J. J., not with G. Mentally I ticket myself for Switzerland, the World Future Conference, thirty years from now. Still, it was G. who, coherent a very few years ago, said to me, "Oh, your fifties are wonderful, wonderful! I never felt better in my life than I did in my fifties. After that it kinda goes downhill."

Do I believe her? I fear I do. I fear. I do. *Over the hill*, what a curiously apt expression after all! The driving and striving slowed, the view superb, you hand off the Sisyphean rock to the person on your left, and, if you're lucky enough to have the health, the means, and the inclination, you stroll down the other side of the alp, working with gravity, gravity working with you. But don't relax; your job now is to put on the brakes a little. Power walk. Don't sit in the wheelchair, the wheels will do what wheels are meant to do. The angel is not always there when you need her, and stepdaughters are notoriously off in Florida.

Tale

Everyone has this story, the tale of the Goblin Obgyn, so it will not be necessary to tell it again, right?

No. True stories are only believed with frequent telling. So here is mine, not so long ago and far away:

When I was forty-five my second marriage ended with the end of his fidelity. I had been happy in the marriage, he hadn't gone out looking for an affair, but it had happened, and my trust had not survived. I had already been through divorce once, and this time I handled it, on the whole, pretty well — understanding that it's harder work to leave than to be left, and that it's easier to end a good relationship than a bad one. All the same, after a month or so I began to bleed and didn't stop for three weeks.

I went to my GP, a gentle and personable intern in family practice. I wasn't willing to go back to Dr. B., the ob-gyn I used to see, I explained, because he had wanted to perform a hysterectomy for no better reason than that, in his opinion, I already had children enough. When I'd told Dr. B. I was not willing to fool around with my psyche in that way, he'd assured me that the loss of a uterus wouldn't bother me. (*Esprit d'escalier*: Shall we cut your balls off then?)

Now Dr. G.P. asked what I was doing to get myself through the divorce. I was keeping busy in the evening, I said, by getting cast in a play. I was recarpeting, for renewal in the house. I was lunching with women friends and driving to the coast every other weekend to be with my younger son in his summer stock company. If I felt I was in trouble, I said, I'd go for counseling.

"People pay thousands of dollars," he cheered me by assuring me, "to learn how to cope like that." All the same, for medical caution, he'd like me to see a gynecologist. There was a new one in town, young, he probably wouldn't give me any nonsense.

At the new Dr. M.'s, the nurse administered a hemoglobin test and stashed me in the cubicle. Dr. M. came in all brisk-and-clipboard, and began to take a medical history. I told him ("me and my big mouth" is the self-deprecatory phrase that comes to mind; in fact I think after all these years I am remarkably trusting, and that this is a virtue not a lack) — why I had not gone back to Dr. B.

"B.'s a good man," he said. "If he wanted to take your womb out, I probably will too." I blanched and held my tongue. When M. got to the advent, in my medical history, of a second dilation and curettage, he said, "Good lord, two D&C's. I'm certainly going to take your womb out. I'm not going to start manipulating you with hormones now!"

"No," I agreed, dry. "But I don't think there's anything wrong with my womb. I think I'm under stress. I'm going through a divorce."

"I know, you're depressed and anxious."

"No," I said, "I'm not. I may be later, but at the moment I'm very active, a bit hyper. It's my usual coping pattern."

"You're depressed and anxious," he repeated, as the nurse came in with the test results. "That's funny. Your blood is normal."

"I'm sure it is," I said. "I think this is a normal reaction to stress, and it'll abate of its own accord."

"I'm the doctor," he actually said. "I'm not interested in the total picture, just my specialty, and then we'll slot it *into* the total picture. It's very clear that what you've got here is dysfunctional bleeding, and you'll need a hysterectomy."

Dysfunctional bleeding? Is that a diagnosis? I thought that's the symptom I came in with. Hysterectomy? We cut out my uterus to slot it into the total picture? Is that some form of medical collage? Dr. M., having diagnosed and prescribed, now left me to undress for the pelvic.

I sat for a minute seething. I powerfully did not want to be touched by his immaculate hands. I had a stabbing awareness of the times in my life when I would not have been able to get mad. I thought: just now it's important for me to feel good about myself. I can't afford the luxury of decorum.

I excused myself to the nurse. "He's made me angry, and I'm not going to have the examination. I'll tell him so myself."

I did so, with surface calm and under-rage. The doctor sat rigid in his dignity. I was minutely mollified that he didn't charge me for the blood test.

Two days later I had a call from my ally Dr. G.P. "I got to thinking about you," he said in his pleasant way, "and I thought maybe we ought to set up an appointment with a psychiatrist just to be sure, because, after all, you must be pretty depressed and anxious."

Bewildered, I let him make the appointment, and it was a half hour later that I tumbled to it, how the boys' network works. This had been one of the few times in my life that I acted, clean and immediate, on anger. I wondered, then, about those two D&C's — were they unnecessary too? — and about the thousands of wombs that were waved away, this way, from women caught more vulnerable than indignant. I wonder now, having learned that flooding is a sign of the climacteric, which stress my body was undergoing, and when the medical establishment will turn its attention to such matters.

Luckily, the following Tuesday (my bleeding having stopped by then), I was able to convince the psychiatrist that I was sane in spite of my unseemly attachment to my uterus.

Stair

Beginning in my teens I used to dream of a house through whose stories I descended carrying a baby in my arms. The staircases would lead to doors that opened into rooms that opened onto staircases ad infinitum. The baby was damaged in some way, club-footed or, more often, wearing the medieval-painting face of an old man. I loved this offspring dearly, and would wake sad at its imperfection.

In my late forties, I dreamed that I had left the baby in the house in Sussex. I went to retrieve it — her? — but the house was full of strangers, tourists somehow, browsing through bric-a-brac for sale on a flagstone terrace above the lawn. The baby was upstairs, but though I could see the stairs I couldn't get to them. Someone said the baby wouldn't know me, and I was abashed, having no evidence it was otherwise.

One reading offered of dreams in general is that both babies and houses are the self, and I can make sense of that. Young, I felt that I carried my deformed self through the labyrinth of my self; middle aged, I went to the self I had left behind to find a portion of my self that no longer claimed me.

Another reading offered is that the dream of babies is a dream of ovum, those that can come to fruit and those that remain a thwarted promise in the body. I can make sense of that, too, the fearful weight of motherhood and then the poignancy of its loss.

But now I am thinking of the stairs. Between the fear of damaged babies and the regret of no more babies, lie thirty-five years of friendship with the woman with whom I have discussed such notions. J. is not my only confidante, but she is the one with whom this particular form of friendship most applies: that we talk the ideas of emotion. We cerebrate about feelings. We are moved by concepts. We analyze impulse. We noeticize sentiment. We fabulate explanation.

And the point is, I never dreamed of friendship. Whatever animal-deep, blood-dark feelings rule my dreams, friendship happened gradually in ordinary light. When J. and I met, it was at a tedious faculty-wives' tea. We got together because of trivial judgment on the local restaurants. We spent the first year over Scrabble, embroidery, TV; and have lived in the same town for only one six-month patch since then.

Often we were apart for years without a phone call or a note, then took the conversation up midsentence. We ran into each other in London, and then it seemed worth the trouble to meet in Belgium, Sussex, Illinois. When I divorced I went where she was. When I went mad she talked me through. When I was happy I discovered that I was telling her the story of my joy. When she went with her family to India I joined them, and we traveled together through Uttar Pradesh ("Oh," we still say in praise of each other's clothes, "it's utter pra-desh!"). When we traveled through the climacteric, it occurred to us that we'd better not let a year go by without meeting somewhere, and now we do — sometimes alone, sometimes with our men in tow, in rental cars and rural restaurants, all four of us willing to honor the longevity of our friendship.

It's my luck that J. is a family therapist, with a certain amount of codified knowledge about the stuff I write. I offer her fiction's insights too. Years ago she showed me her "stair graph" of intimate relationship. People approach each other in the form of two facing staircases. At first they're far apart on the topmost tread; each takes a tentative step forward, toward the other. Then each descends into herself/himself, and if it seems worth the risk, the effort, takes another step. As long as they keep going into themselves and coming forward, the relationship gets deeper and closer, and can do so till death, though the stairs will never meet. If either refuses either motion, to plumb the self or face the other, the symmetry is skewed and the relationship will strain or break.

We were talking at the time, it will surprise no one to learn, about male-female relationships, and in particular the skewed-asymmetrical-strained quality of my own. The stair graph is a kind of image I can keep in mind even when I am dealing with bifurcating chaos in the gut; and it signally helped me in the area for which she intended it.

Only lately it occurs to me that J. and I, ourselves, have demonstrated her graph, apart and together, delving into our selves and bringing forward what we've found; and that — for all the ova come and gone in our reproductive lives — we've created something that our subconsciouses did not warn us would be the stuff of life. Mating and maternity are in the blood; I have carried babies downstairs and gone upstairs to fetch them both literally and figuratively all the years of my adulthood. But no one is more clearly family to me than J.

In India it happened that we arrived at Fatehpur Sikri on the Feast of Id. I have a snapshot of the two of us, J. and I, backgrounded by the brilliantly silk-swathed stalls, Laurel and Hardy in build, bare-armed and sweating in 110 degrees of Indian July, grinning ourselves toward each other down the ancient steps, old girls in an invented kinship, one step forward, one step down.

Hell

I wake under a feather duvet in a red cover, slightly jet-lagged. My stomach is clenched in a sickness of fear, which slowly reveals itself to be attached to something silly, a phone call I have to make, a repair to be seen to. My back aches too, and will never again *not* protest against an overnight airplane seat, so that this connection of travel and pain is a permanent feature remaining to my life. The fear sits sick, and spreads. Something about London, the bombardment from every side of ambition and accomplishment, the failure of socialism, the homeless on the corner, the posturing of heads of state. My own inadequacy. In a while I will get up, have coffee, do my exercises, have a nice day. Not yet.

In my middle forties I went through a period of two years in which I would wake and rage. The fury was unpredictable in its target. There was always something to attach it to — an imagined slight, a real injustice, an irremediable wound from the past. I resigned myself to the condition as permanent, something I had to endure because it was a part of me, probably the fruits of having repressed my anger for so long. Then I stopped drinking alcohol, adopted HRT, and wasn't angry anymore.

Now usually I wake with anticipation, admire the plaster rose on my London ceiling or the real banana tree beyond P.'s Florida sliding door, which seems to give off the scent of the coffee he will bring me in a minute. Early-morning moods are rare, and I no longer believe they will outlast the comics page, let alone the calendar. But on the infrequent occasions when the dark ambushes me, it is not as anger but as dread; it takes me by surprise and hits with force.

I have no way of knowing what changes in my body, psyche, spirit, for gain or loss, have to do with menopause, and which have to do with aging, or both, or how much of each. Jet lag, diet, muscle spasm, hormones — I consult the possibilities blind; I recognize recurrent feelings but I can't really judge what comes from situation, what from chemistry. Why should the black mood represent imbalance anyway, instead of simple insight? How much honesty is there in despair? How much of a figment is my usual busy cheer? Here, dark before dawn, muffled in feathers, how much more truth may I touch than in a day of doing?

A statistical analysis on page four of yesterday's *Guardian* shows that pessimistic people have a more realistic view than optimists, both of probabilities and of their own control over events. Optimists, however, *take* better control, and therefore accomplish more. Ergo, self-deception is functional.

When I was in college in the late fifties, in New York, I bought (from a bargain rack, it must have been, because I was too poor for new hardback books) Katherine Anne Porter's memoir *The Days Before*. The only memory of it I now retain is the pencil-soft portrait on the cover and Porter's observation that we trust hate more than love. Love we think needs to be coaxed and nurtured, carefully maintained. Whereas impulses of contempt have the force of permanent truth. "I love you" is always subject to review. "I hate you" comes from the core.

Mostly, I have taken her observation as admonition. Why should we grant hate such force? Why should we think love so fragile when there's so much evidence of its resilience?

But isn't the answer simply: entropy? Both eros and agape shatter like a cup knocked on the floor. In some far future when "future" is reversed, the universe contracts, and the past is yet to come, then the cup will jump back on the table and repair itself, hate will need fertilizer pellets, and love will cover the world like kudzu. But I can't imagine such a future, let alone believe in it, and in the meantime affection is fragile, compassion delicate. We are clumsy, ravenous, and short of time.

The image of E. looms as I last saw her, her fierce despair and her cantankerous kindness. We said good-bye on the sill of the Sussex house she was about to lose to taxes, and that was before her paralysis as a writer, before morphine addiction, ten years before she died at 92. My own life may seem to have come round to peace and safety. All the same, the rule is: death.

Abruptly I am off on my death run, worried for my friends, the world. I think X.'s health precarious, and R. lives a gray half-life. Y. may certainly have AIDS. Z. drinks too much, and Q. consumes herself protecting him. How fragile and out of control we are. I would touch wood, but that's too solid. Touch paper, touch leaf, touch cobweb.

I'm surrounded with people (young, but of my own age too) who think the race will muddle through; that sense will solve the population problem, technology restore the rain forests and the ozone layer, good will cope with the economy. What evidence supports such hope? Liberal democracy has triumphed and sells itself like laundry soap. Ethnic autonomy turns out to be bloody nationalism. England (England!) is pissing away its universities. Money represents not production but rumors of more money. This is not a recession, says J. It is the end of the world as we've (gluttonously) known it.

Serbia! Sarejevo! We have not given a thought to little Bosnia-Herzegovina for seventy-eight years, except I understand that the Orient Express went through, and the rugs were a splendid bargain. Bosnian refugees now are being processed through the Austrian camps through which P. and his family moved after World War II. The lice are still there. "Ethnic cleansing" fights for front-page space with the incipient collapse of Michael Jackson's plastic face. What do we learn? Are we worth saving?

Dread floods me like a hot flush. I see this will be one of those days dogged by clumsiness and tender skin. I will be too large, mincing, magnet to objects at the level of my thighs. No, I'll be all right. I'll be better once I've had coffee, done my exercises, made that call.

Not yet.

Heal

I have no memory of stepping wrong off a boulder in the Chiricahuas. I was looking at the canyon, the climb of trees on the other side, the rim of stones like crumbling columns too tight-packed to fall — and the next thing I knew I was ass to the ground, one hand around a wrench of pain in my left ankle and the other clamping a palm full of flesh to the right knee. I figured the ankle was the more serious but that only an Xray would see how serious. The knee I took a look at, prizing my hand off by centimeters.

Pretty bad. The width of my kneecap, a deep scalloped flap like an upside-down cloud shape, cloud-pale but seeping blood around the edges — and is that bone, that bit? I'm aware not only of hurt and pounding heart but of incipient and protracted nuisance. Poor P. He'll have to look after me. He won't mind, but I'll be tense with apology. Our poor vacation, we'll hobble through the rest. Poor me. This is going to take a long time.

Hand clamped to the knee, blood seeping, I don't realize how long I've been there until I hear P. calling.

"Jesus, why didn't you yell?"

I'm embarrassed to tell him I was embarrassed to have hurt myself.

It's children who are supposed to be repositories of awe. I don't think so. I think that children accept the natural miracles, and are dazzled only once they have a rudimentary notion of how things work, by things that appear not to — magic, cartoons, fireworks, "effects" that are some way "special." I know that when I was little and skinned my knee, I took it as no great gift that the wound would sting and bleed. I endured the knowledge that my mother would get the dirt out whether I screamed about it or was brave. I knew it would stanch, and scab, and itch, and knit itself, probably with a little scar.

At fifty-five I watch this process with exploding wonder. It happens at wizard speed. The ankle produces its egg swelling within a couple of hours. I can walk on it next day, well enough to perambulate the border into Mexico, to shop for trinkets including a handsome carved cane. It's clear after all no bone is broken, and over the weeks as the swelling recedes it leaves a ring of delicate blue posies around my heel, which gradually like posies fade. The cut is an angry ruck of skin, which sucks itself back to its bed so hard that bending the knee becomes my major problem. I find I am fighting not the hurt but the healing, stretching against the eagerness of my flesh to knit. The blood fists into a dark scab, goes drab, and begins to lift around the edges. The shallower cut at each side of the kneecap smooths and flattens. Within a month, back in Florida in tepid Gulf salt water, I lose the scab and emerge from the ocean whole, just a slight, double, raised pink bloom on my knee, which looks a little tender, though it isn't.

My question is: why, when — even after a half-century, and after its ability to reproduce itself is past — a body not particularly well looked after will demonstrate its enthusiasm for survival in such wise, will speed goods about the veins, pump blood and antibodies, set itself to coagulation, osmosis, cleansing, and creation, will mend so thoroughly that mobility and convenience are restored that could not be had from half a ton of technology — why, I say, should I ever have bitterly blamed it for such trifles as I have blamed it for: for having too much flesh in this spot, too little muscle in that, for producing this wrinkle, that sag, that gray hair, or this texture? Dear body! My dear body! It has gone about its incessant business with very little thanks.

I wake from a dream of D. We were having tea in a pleasantly shabby Victorian room, books and papers jumbled everywhere. "What are you going to do next?" I asked, and she said, "Nothing."

"Ah." I was a little disconcerted.

"Yes," she said. "I worked so hard early on that I feel I was cheated of my youth. What would you do, if you were going to make up for a lost youth?"

She seemed to want my answer. "I'd get a good masseur," I said. "I'd have a good hard workout, and then a really deep massage."

"I never thought of that." She paid me a look of keen attention.

"Yes, and then I'd dance. I'd read of course, and so forth. But, definitely, I'd dance."

Waking, I know that I've been blatantly giving me good advice in my sleep. I giggle, reach my fingers out in a balletic gesture, meaning to touch P.'s back, but my forearm tumbles off the edge of the single bed, into the void under the red duvet. Oh yes. Another week before I'm back in Florida.

Okay. A week of friends and work. My ceiling rose is very pretty. I wrap myself for comfort, and in the hazy sleep-light I remember another quilt, the blue chintz with the cotton satin border that my grandmother made when I was — six? It was kapok filled, the stuffing held in place by yarn ties; I remember her plump fingers pulling tight the knots.

There is a photograph of me on that quilt, spread on the spiky brown grass in front of the house on Alvarado Street. I am on my stomach, arms stiff in front of me, pointed toe touching my forehead over my arched back. I am ringletted like Shirley Temple, wearing a blue ruffled satin dance dress with tiny straps.

I remember, too, the buying of that costume, a miracle out of a rummage sale, one sleepy dawn when there was still such a thing as a vacant lot in downtown Phoenix, and the Women's Society for Christian Service had filled it with church tables covered in white paper and old clothes. I wandered among the rows while my mother sorted castoffs that black and Mexican women waited in the hot dark to buy, for small change that the church would send to Africa.

I remember discovering the satin slip of a ruffled dress, pulling it out of a jumble of plaid cotton and scratchy wools. I remember my fear that some other mother would buy it before I could convince my own; and the hot quarter mom slipped into my palm, which I handed over to the church lady behind the table — for satin, for ruffles. For a snapshot of a pose on the chintz quilt.

There are also photographs of me in pastel taffeta for the Gene Bumph revue, with silver sparkles on the yoke and a tilted pancake hat held in place by tight elastic; in a variegated fall of silk chiffon — turquoise, azure, emerald — when I danced a piece of seaweed to Ruth St. Denis's octopus; in patent leather tap shoes with glossy bows and silver heels; in a pink tutu; in a red satin bum-skimmer skirt with white band jacket, gold Lurex frogs.

How I wanted to dance! And how persistently my body announced itself unfit for such endeavor. Apologizing for the extravagance of my lessons, Mom would laugh, "I've got to do something about her, she's so clumsy!" Nor did this register as a cruelty, for I also thought our mutual desire was hubris. I was the stage child of a stage mother. I sat in the dark recital halls and made Shirley Temple moues.

At home my brother grunted while I practiced acrobatics on the living room rug. Chestrolls, backbends. *Amos 'n' Andy* played on the radio; Dad sat at once inert and intent, because he loved a good "show." My mother darned. I did headstands with my head on a cushion and my hands positioned for a tripod; I did elbow stands with my soles against the door, while my brother sat on the couch mocking, saying: *Ugh! Ugh! I can do that too!*

There were toe shoes, little wads of lambswool, pain; and the satin ribbons crossed up my calves frenetically, as if I could will myself into a prima. There was a sheer rig in an autumnal theme, in the synthetics that had come in by then, skimpy on my solid prepubescent frame.

There was the hateful, garish jester's costume when I became too thick for acrobatics and was cast as the physical equivalent of a straight man in what they dignified with the name "Adagio."

Wrong body, wrong body. I gave up the lessons, finally. I went to the North High basketball dances and stood in a corner in flocked nylon, praying for anybody to ask me onto the floor. I learned to jitterbug, defiant, and took a prize at it with my brother's college roommate. I learned to twist in time to chaperon my first college students. Once, in my thirties, for a lark, I threw a party and hired a dancer to come teach us all to disco.

My body, my poor body. When was it I learned to put on a tape and dance for me?

I stretch my ankle into a gingerly *pointe*, finger the polished scar. I think: dying, we heal. Over the hill, both body and psyche are still scrambling after order for themselves.

I know this. I learned very late why my love affairs ended in diminishment and recrimination. It's a long story that I can tell in a phrase or two. I always chose men I could not please. I worked very hard to understand this, and finally I understood it. I worked very hard to change, and eventually I changed. Bit by bit my psyche coagulated, scabbed, and knit.

Now I bend my knee, caress its fresh bloom. The costumes turn in my mind, cutouts of photographs, afloat. They tumble around me in a slow free fall. They are all there, the bows and the spangles, the chiffons wafting, the satin ruffles; they are putting me back to sleep. My duvet lifts and begins to lose its color. It pales and floats as a cloud would float, unsupported in the middle air. Around me, Chagall-like, Aunt J. J. and W. go power walking on a nimbus. G.'s wheelchair spins, J. is skipping down a stair, E. is rocking back and forth over her Sussex sill. The world's a long way down.

I learned an interesting fact about detachment. Apparently the reason leaves fall is that as summer ends they suddenly produce a burst of fresh growth. They're so productive that the join at the matrix near the branch is weak. Then even a slight wind will break them off.

J. said that older people find it necessary to detach, and do so in myriad ways. They get deaf, they don't remember. They relive their lives, go quiet, go inward, concentrating on self. Dying and healing in tandem, they go about the natural, necessary business of letting go.

This process is hardly begun in me. I have loving yet to do. But I know what it means, I feel the beginning of it, on my cloud duvet. I have nearly learned that I can't control what happens in the world. I've nearly understood that I don't have to. I have nearly got it, that my friends and I are going to die, and that whether the planet offs itself will be decided without particular reference to me. I can do a little, and I'm responsible for the little I can do. I can give X. a call tomorrow, recycle my trash, for instance. I can value P. and celebrate my scar.

That's all. That's all I can do, and all I am required to do. In the gray half-light of sleep I climb my duvet to dance.

Trash Talk

When's the last time you saw Mickey Mouse in a story line? Name a narrative conflict he's confronted since that broom and bucket in *Fantasia*. That was *1940*!

Describe a typical Mickey activity.

You know who says, "What's up, doc?" and "Th-that's all, folks," and "Beep-beep!" But what is Mickey's favorite line of dialogue?

His theme parks have a theater apiece devoted to him, where the program never changes, and *that* movie has a plot — the humble beginnings, the evolution of mouse outline on the drawing board, the Horatio Alger rise: Mickey's is the story of the content-free success. His spheroid ears are everywhere, his quadra-digit gloves, his plumber's-friend shoes. What does he do?

Nuttin'. He's a logo and an icon, he has no self but instant recognizability; the perfect star, fabulous beyond Fabbio at being famous for his fame. His function is to sell T-shirts, spills 'n' thrills, and time-share real estate; and what he sells is always Mickey Mouse. He's the capitalist 'toon tautology, advertising chasing itself up its own ass to the bank.

I don't remember why we were discussing religion on the way back from Disney World. The road signs, probably. Anne was asleep in the backseat. Peter said, "You have to have a religion that looks to an afterlife for happiness, before you can justify abusing the earth." Peter is a lapsed Catholic, and when challenged to sum his identity in one word, *lapsed* was the word he chose.

What he said now put me in mind of David Daiches, my old supervisor at Cambridge, who one afternoon observed that there's a good deal of self-regard in a religion "in which the *summum bonum* is the salvation of one's own soul."

It reminded me, too, of Doris Lessing, in *Prisons We Choose to Live Inside*, saying that Christianity has dictated the pattern of Western political thought: *we live in a vale of tears now, but if we follow the Messiah we will find perfect bliss. Believe in The Word and all will be transformed.*

The thing is, it's not just politics. It's also the way we sell soap and shoes.

My first experience of fund-raising occurred in the old Central Methodist Church in Phoenix, Arizona. The building was a massive stucco cube in a stolid style I have since come to associate with Masonic temples. Its sanctuary was plain as a garage, and the Reverend Charles S. Kendall had hired a professional fund-raiser to leaven enough money out of us to build a grander church. This hiring was unheard-of-modern, and rather thrilled us all. I was about ten, a Sunday school regular, when the campaign began. A plywood thermometer ten feet high appeared beside the altar, where Sunday night services were given over to the professional man. The thermometer was marked off in amounts of money. Somebody painted in the red gauge as the fund-raiser whipped us auctioneer-style into a turbulence of generosity.

In my memory these sessions have the atmosphere of The Little Engine That Could. Could we raise enough money for a Spanish tile roof? An eighty-foot spire? A stained glass rose window? We thought we could. Every week my parents dug into their pockets and upped their pledge. We thought we could. I saved my allowance and returned coke bottles for extra pennies. We thought we could.

I was at once bored, titillated, and absolutely trustful of this process. I remember noting that if the stuff in the thermometer at home should burst out the end, it would mean something dire; but here, now, the red ejaculation was devoutly to be desired.

I'm a lapsed Methodist moralist. I am what Elizabeth Bowen meant, I suppose, by a "pious agnostic." I believe we have some fundamental obligations of behavior without believing that there is any cosmic intelligence making such requirements. I am rather righteous about God's being beyond our understanding, and I accept the likelihood that the Absolute is chemical. Job's my book, and Ecclesiastes — though I confess I have, in troubled times, leaned on a psalm or two.

Meanwhile I am also one of those who profess literature as a religion, conscious that the writing trade has its own temptations — schisms, superstition, sects, fundamentalism, and money changers in the temple. Conscious also that the Theorists have a sound and deeply troubling point. All language is conservative, they say; it emanates from the empowered to preserve the status quo. I am uncomfortably conscious that like all the faithful I have tended to credit my god with a freedom from local influence it may not possess.

Still, it is through writing that I have been able, just, to understand the concept of a God at once personal and omnipotent — that is, I see that I love my villainous characters no less than my heroes, and often more. I am willing that all of them should suffer in order to learn. I celebrate a system that includes their disease, decay, and death.

I also believe in the moral use of written words, as a vehicle for the capacity humans have of imagining each other. I think this capacity is urgently in need just now, in the societal pastiche we do and will inhabit. If the tyrannies of language betray us, we had better imagine one another more carefully, and more frequently.

Literature is my credo because it is capacious, tentative, and empathetic; because it acknowledges irony and anomaly; because it poses dilemmas, for which it declines to offer a way out, in small acts of perpetual reconciliation.

It was at Central Methodist, too, that I learned the fundamentals of self-promotion. My mother was an elocution teacher, and I was a regular sayer of "pieces" for the Friday night potluck socials. (*My darling little goldfish / Hasn't any toes*, etc.)

I learned from these efforts two lessons: that I should try as hard as possible to make people praise me, and that when they did I should say it was nothing much.

It was a shock when I entered college to encounter Beowulf, that first trash talker of the canon, vaunting for the glory of Christ.

In my youth I have set about many great deeds . . . bloody from my foes, I came from the fight where I had bound five, destroyed a family of giants, and at night in the waves slain water-monsters . . . ground enemies to bits . . .

These evenings I think of Beowulf as I strain to read the lips of the NBA badboys dribbling upcourt — Reggie Miller and John Starks,

Vernon Maxwell, Scottie Pippin. I fantasize that if I could only decipher it, I'd hear some form of poetry appropriate to swagger, muscles, fleet feet, and feats of derring-do.

I like other forms of bragging also. Dad had a keen eye for billboard chic and clever signs. We used to point them out to each other on the way to California: Curry's Mile-Hi cones, the Coppertone toddler with the doggie exposing her pale bum. Dad believed with Elmer Rice that you should "sell the sizzle," but we had a genetic disposition to think that irony sold sizzle best. Jingles were good. Burma Shave was the pinnacle, for its whimsy.

I feel this way still: I admire an ad that self-destructs. The British win hands down; they tongue their cheeks, mock beer with Shakespeare, make you puzzle out what brand name the picture represents. My favorite was a TV spot for Cadbury's Instant Mash: it showed and described a real potato: *Sort of lumpy, you have to wash the dirt off, peel it, boil it, mash it; it's good, but it'll never catch on.*

Dad taught me to appreciate a nifty gimmick and a tooting patter. But he himself was not adept at self-promotion. He was likely to point out the flaws in his house plans. To the client! *You might have drainage problems; the bathroom's too small, really; if I put the closet here, you'll have to walk around the hall.* It drove my mother nuts. *Don't say what's wrong with it!*

The rules were different, I speculated, for house plans and elocution pieces. Or for grown-ups and children. Or for girls and men? Or for things you got paid for and things you did for free?

My last experience of fund-raising was in the late eighties. I was on the board of a national writer's group whose NEA grant had been cut by more than half, some $35,000. Then the NEA turned around and gave us an "advancement" grant for the same amount, which was not paid to us but to a Madison Avenue PR consultant to teach us how not to be so dependent.

As co-veep I joined the director in New York for the seminars. The quarters of the consultancy were very high tech, very plush. There were electronic doors and automatic dimmer lights, though the AC had gone awry and it was too cold for the computerized controls, so the lights kept dimming and the doors kept swishing open and closed at high-tech random.

There were a hundred or so in attendance. I have some notes. The first instructor told us that although we were in the arts, "In this country we all end up in sales." He told us, whatever we had to say, to "boil it down to a sentence." He told us, "It never hurts to write a personal note to people you don't know personally."

Next, a woman I have noted as Headmistress of Advancement enlightened us about "market mindset." She told us that if we wanted to do our damnedest for the arts, we would "get in there and slug it out with the rest of the corporations." She said "sophisticated targeting" and "randomly selected stratified phone survey" and "motivation perception" and "blips you can play off of." She asked us to write down what we *really* cared for. Desperate, I wrote: *Language.* She asked us to write down what, in our wildest dreams, would be the target expansion of our organization at the end of the next five years.

I think I either resigned or was fired from the board when I wrote, and showed the director that I had written, "I think we're just about the right size now."

A man named Halsey North came on. He had a boyish bounce. He reminded me of the Reverend Charles S. Kendall back at Central. Halsey North said, "In speaking of strategy, I use the analogy of a church, which will employ many kinds of mechanism to give its congregation a sense of ownership."

All religions demand brand loyalty. Each method is the only method, each Word the only Word. But the Jesus message itself was ambiguous; on the one hand, *I am the way and the light,* on the other, *seek poverty, suffer the little children, the meek shall inherit.*

In America we have chosen only the opening shot of this. Christianity and Capitalism meet in the figure of the television evangelist, through the agent of self-promotion. The medium is the Messiah. Swaggart, Bakker, et al. are cartoons of our national character, and it may be that the greatest harm they do is to provide us with a caricature from which we can distance ourselves, thus denying our complicity.

I got a letter that greeted me "Dear Friend and Fan," from somebody I may have met once, I don't know, telling me how her new novel (from a very major publisher!) was "exuberant, comic, written in lively prose that combines feminism, eroticism, satire and the supernatural. . . ." She hoped I would find it as stimulating to read as she did to write.

Gosh, I envy her. I would never be able to hope for my readers that they find the reading of my novel as long, angst-ridden, despairing, enlivened by moments of hope, boring, intermittently happy, stimulating, dogged, and drudging, as it was for me. There's no *way* it would be worth their while to read.

Every now and again I find myself in range of a rangy postmodernist computer-and-mall warrior — there's one in the summer 1993 *AWP Chronicle*, Martin Schecter — and am skewered as a romantic modernist liberal with tenure and a big mortgage (yup, that's got me) — and then this same warrior goes off scattershot in such a screech of ital. and caps, exclamation marks and rhetorical questions ("What these Guardians of Nostalgia need to do is come down from their Romantic-Modernist high horse . . . we never stop hearing from all these people who've 'made it' just how aesthetically 'pure' and 'uninfluenced' their aesthetic is, and how 'competitive' and 'entrepreneurial' the youngsters are . . . why not join us? Join us and have fun and make money and not worry about it . . .") that I sorta reconstruct myself, flow back together like a computer special effect, murmuring *Heigh ho, Silver. . . .*

In the past year policy mandates have been spewing and spilling forth from the administration of my university, demanding that the department should justify its faculty to the bottom line. We have been asked for several thousand pages of enhanced vitae, testimonials, mission statements, recommendations, reviews, revisions, reaccreditations, proofs of productivity, and evidence of visibility. That is, promo, puffs, PR, self-aggrandizement, vaunts, hype, and trash talk. *Don't say what's wrong with it!*

It's the old issue of God and Mammon, of course, but it isn't just that our Madonna is a material girl, it's that our language has seduced us, the wielders of it. We are engaged in a universal grade inflation, and we believe the rhetoric of our own letters of recommendation. Not only in business and politics but in education, law, the social services, and the arts, we can't separate the rhetoric of ethics from the rhetoric of the ad. It's a question of what's "good." M-m-good. It's Good America. It's the Real Thing. Just do it. Progress is our most important. When you care enough. New and improved. Better living. I love what you do for me.

This mangling of language mangles thought; it leads us into deception. It leads us to believe that Nixon, Reagan, Coke, and Nike can render us safe, affluent, sexy, and strong. Not necessarily in that order.

What's my point? Nothing is easier than trashing Mickey Mouse. Mickey Mammon Mouse Messiah. We are driving home from Disney World in spiffing new T-shirts; Anne has ears. There's one terrific series of billboards for a motel chain, family whimsy gags, grandson of Burma-Shave. I live a nice middle-class life; I'm not saying otherwise.

What is it I want to salvage out of romantic modernism?

This: a kind of blunt dumb honesty about what we make and do. Art is long, for example. It's lonely. It hurts your family time. Fiction is a godlike undertaking, and also nothing much. Most of it ends up in the trash either before or after publication. I want back a smidgeon of meekitude. I want gender equality by living with a man who will describe himself as *lapsed*. I want the tentative; *self* accompanied by *-irony* as often as *-promotion*; trash talk that can take the mickey out of its own best brag.

I once had an actor friend who'd landed the role of a sculptor in a play full of reality-and-illusion dialogue, philosophical ranting, bombast about death, soul, and transcendence. The actor called me to complain that the playwright had skipped town for the weekend, leaving him with "a rewrite with seven fucking prepositions in a single sentence! Have you ever fucking tried to say a fucking sentence with seven fucking prepositions in it?"

That, I thought, had an authentic ring. I understood his spiritual values.

My One True West . . . .

know a lanky Hungarian who was six years old when his family
was ejected by the Communists —

Wait. I'm going to show you the true West.

— from their vineyards in the village of Mucsi south of Budapest in 1947, and was shunted train by train across Austria, Switzerland, and Germany East and West; lived for three years in
the medieval Rhineland town of Eltville, and then, debriefed in a
camp at Bremen where they were interrogated, inoculated, and always
hungry, emigrated to Milwaukee.

Wait.

This Displaced Person, hereinafter referred to as DP — not his true
name — took his image of America from Westerns shown circa 1948–
51 in a movie theater converted from a gabled house next to a soccer
field along the Rhine, absorbed them with such a force of longing that
he arrived in Wisconsin saying "yessir" and "pardner" and grew up to
be a cinema critic and professor of film although he never got to Arizona until, the summer we were both fifty, I took him home.

Now.

We are traveling I-10 coast to coast in a rented Continental like a rolling
living room. It is quiet with the windows up, and we talk a lot. Remembering other Texas crossings — in an aqua '44 Plymouth, a square,
white '50 Ford, a two-tone Dodge with fins — I warn him that Texas
is the width of purgatory, and that before we get across he will come
to believe it will never end. But it turns out this isn't so. There had been
no interstate under those old cars, and now as soon as the Houston ex-
its are behind us the signs to San Antonio start overhead. The miles fall
under the excellent suspension of our armchairs, and we are armed
against the wilderness with childhood memories and tapes of Leonard

Cohen and the voice of Cokie Roberts considering all things. Derricks like behemoths bob interestingly on the horizon. Texas has had a wet winter, so the great plain is bubbling with green scrub. Palo verde drips its leaves over the meridian.

Oh, no, he says, this isn't desert; it's much too lush.

In Phoenix when I was a girl we had one squat palm, one bitter orange, and an oleander hedge. The grass stabbed at your soles like straw. I sat in the sandbox and broke off an oleander leaf, feeling morally contaminated because I had been told not to, feeling queasy at the viscous drip of poison milk, the thought of that contaminating white slime on my tongue. The sand was no earthly use. All you could make of it was a mound that slid dry down its own sides. The hose wouldn't reach. I brought a glass of water all the way from the kitchen sink, slopping it from the porch, across the hot gravel drive. Hoping for castles, I poured it in the sandbox, where it sank without a trace.

DP could hear the bombs, maybe south toward the city of Pécs or as near as Dómbóvár ten miles away. But he saw no fighting, no death, and not a single gun. He never heard the word *Nazi*, though he knew that his father disliked Russians. When he got to Eltville he was seven; the children mocked him as a dirty DP if he spoke Hungarian, as a gypsy if he slipped into the Mucsi dialect. John Wayne appeared out of dusty nowhere, the outsider, horseless, carrying his saddle and his rifle. He climbed out the window and swung to the buckboard, he defended the ladies with his life; he saved the whole stagecoach of humanity from the Indians, who were the enemy. The most important position you could have, DP inferred, was riding shotgun.

New Mexico and Arizona have had a wet winter too. We pass through Lordsburg on cruise control, and I am nervous about the verdant stubble of what ought to be cowboy dirt. There are fields DP claims are wheat. I assure him hotly that this is impossible. But a few miles along we arrive at a sign clearly set there for our benefit, since *WHEAT* is all it says. Tucson is full of roses. The saguaro forest is swollen green. NPR tells us that the pollen count is higher than Florida's. In Tombstone we buy Doc Holliday posters and sip a Heineken at the OK Corral Saloon in AC brought down to sixty-five degrees.

Not here, he says.

In Phoenix in the forties only the rich had air-conditioning, but we had a "damp air cooler" based on the principle of sweat: six thicknesses of hairy insulation sat in a metal box on the garage rafters, under a pipe that trickled water all day long. A fan blew across with enough force to push the air through ducts into the rooms. Dampened air took the temperature down ten or fifteen degrees, which meant, in high summer, down to eighty-five or ninety.

Out of the sky four total annual inches fell, maybe eight or a dozen hours out of the year. The kids ran in the gutter, splashing up over the rolling curbs on bikes, screaming. The one time it snowed they closed the schools even though the flakes disappeared before they hit concrete.

I lived from water to water. From the freezing metal trays at Virginia Tweedy's house across shade patch and asphalt to the spigot beside the porch. From the root beer float at MacAlpine Drugs to the thermos of lemonade beside the lagoon at Encanto Park. If it was later than March and earlier than November, you could stick the hose in a fifty-gallon barrel and climb in. Real summer smelled like the Monte Vista munic-ipal swimming pool, with its steamy bodies in the changing room, the basket with the numbered diaper pin to check my clothes, the wad-ing pool of disinfectant by the door, the life-giving stench of chlorine, the toes on the tile, the deep breath, the plunge. The Pacific Ocean ex-isted for only two weeks in July and had to be got to by pilgrimage across the Mojave Desert, preferably before dawn so vapor lock didn't strand you at El Centro. Then ocean boiled up cold on the sand at Long Beach, Laguna, and Del Mar, smelling of fish and petroleum. It was, like newborn kittens, like escalators, something impossible to be-lieve in except when you were looking right at it. I looked right at it, from where it simmered over my feet to where it disappeared over the rim of the world.

DP's father was conscripted into the Hungarian army one summer early in the war. He lasted two weeks in boot camp, then he deserted, escaped, returned to the village of Mucsi, and went back to harvesting the grapes. When the Germans occupied Hungary, he was conscripted into the Nazi army and sent to boot camp. He took along his Hungarian uniform. When he deserted two weeks later he made his way back to Mucsi by changing his clothes, wearing the Hungarian uniform in German territory, German in Hungarian. He hollowed out a haystack and slept in it for most of the next two years. For him, war smelled like fermenting grass.

When the family got to East Germany, the Communist authorities ordered DP's father into the coal mines, and he escaped across the border to the west. A priest uncle came with false papers to smuggle DP out. A second uncle came with a second set of false papers to smuggle his little brother. There was no one left to rescue the women, so DP's mother and his thirteen-year-old sister walked out on their own. When the family reunited, DP took hold of his mother's skirt and didn't let go for three weeks.

In Eltville, DP says, there was a brown beetle that loved the chestnut trees, fed on them, and fell from them — a segmented, friendly bug. He would put one in the sliding tray of a matchbox, stuff it in his pocket, and go to the movies to see Hopalong Cassidy and Bob Steele. From time to time he would take out the matchbox and look at his bug. If it got out and crawled in his pocket, that was okay. Tom Mix and Hopalong were tall, but Bob Steele was a little, feisty guy, fists pumping all the time in self-defense and in defense of right and justice.

We dawdle in Crystal Cove, looking for sea urchins in the tidal pools. The rocks have tumbled each other into pastel chips. It's very late when we get back to our hotel in Laguna, settle down to a room service hamburger, and flip on, no kidding, *Gunfight at the O.K. Corral*.

Look at all that green! I say. There's scrub and chaparral in every shot!

He admits it. Those early Westerns were in black and white, so the whole gray landscape translated in his head to brown. By the time Technicolor came along he had the fixed conviction that nothing grew out here.

The swinging glass doors of the Phoenix Orpheum had a penguin decal, wings outstretched and icicles on his wings: *20 Degrees Cooler Inside*. It was a full-scale movie palace, the auditorium a Spanish courtyard with clouds projected scudding overhead. I didn't like Westerns and didn't watch them unless I came in in the middle and had to wait through the double feature. Why would I want to look at scrub and cactus when I could see them out the door?

I went for Shirley Temple, top hats, tap dancing, and pathos. Later I liked the swoony fulfillment of absolute romance. I wasn't picky as to style — Katharine Hepburn, Rita Hayworth, Grace Kelly, Doris Day. I could plot the rise of romantic expectation in my shivering digestive tract. For decades afterward I blamed my messy life on having bought the whole Hollywood caboodle about Mr. Right. Then it occurred to me that the lesson was a little askew to that. It wasn't so much that all those leading ladies found the perfect mate, but that they found a perfect mate in Cary this week, Jimmy next, Gregory a few months on and Rock or Jeffrey after that. Hollywood might have meant to be preaching Mr. Right, but the underlying message was serial monogamy.

But Westerns are full of bullshit too, I say. Even apart from the gun-fights, and savaging the Apaches — all that kissing horses and off into the sunset.

Oh, sure.

What is it you learned from them then?

The usual things, he says. The outsider wears the white hat. Be kind to animals and loyal to your friends. Defend the women with your life. Be suspicious of bankers and businessmen.

We're almost there.

Tell me again, I say.

I think they taught me authenticity. My guess is that Sartre spent a lot of time watching Westerns.

Not Sartre; you.

Me too. The loner is an existential hero. Stand up for what you believe. Be steadfast. Be direct. No lies. Suspect civilization, but make community with strangers where you can. Look for a livable Utopia.

Now.

It isn't easy to find your One True West in a culture as mobile and multi as this one. (Mom would have said: *Hungarian?*) You have to go several thousand miles and part way back again. The True West wasn't made in heaven. You have to buy into the myth and then revise it till it suits you.

Here.

We find it on a stretch of two-lane between the California border and Yuma. The desert floor undulates as if the ocean has washed it up for millennia. It's milky brown, unbroken to the swell of the butte that lifts red sandstone against an eye-blue sky. There isn't a scrap of green and no living thing to be seen moving in the basin.

Yep, he says. Here it is.

The lookout point is on the wrong side of the road, so we dodge the trucks at sixty-five miles an hour across, DP carrying the videocam.

I never would've thought it would be Yuma, I say. I always hated Yuma.

He hoists the videocam and tapes one-handed, aiming in every direction, riding shotgun. It's a perfect hundred degrees and breathless brown, and butte, and blue.

Yuma! I marvel.

But this is it, doncha think, pardner?

Yessir, I say. I do.

Freeze Frame

remarried, and I rearranged the photographs. The tintypes of my grandparents would stay on the kitchen wall, but Peter's should be added; one of the great-aunts could come down in favor of my new stepdaughter, Anne; we must put up current snaps of the boys in their African and London lairs. My brother, too, had remarried; his late wife should be laid away.

In the storeroom I found an odd-sized frame that was, oddly, just right for the best Christmas shot of Peter, Anne, and me: a rectangle five inches by nine, in which we stood with our arms loosely tangled in front of the bedecked door, looking for all the world like an established family. The frame was elegant deco, antiqued gilt with a swirl of vaguely oriental decoration. It held a studio portrait of my stepmother's father, a Mr. Srofe — if I once knew his first name it was gone — a man I never met and about whom I knew only two things: that he died long and tortuously of Alzheimer's, and that in better times he was a pioneer artisan of American packaging. In the thirties and forties he did industrial origami, inventing ways to fold a piece of cardboard so that it would hold a naked tube upright or untwist to reveal a nest of malted balls. I have seen scrapbooks of his Prells and Vaselines. He made octagons for bubble bath and paper prosceniums for cologne.

I set to opening his frame with a pair of screwdrivers and a needle-nosed pliers. Most of the frames I own are new and cleverly designed. Several come apart with the flipping of four tabs; one slides asunder with a single swivel. But Mr. Srofe was not packaged for easy disassembly. The backing was a piece of cardboard gilded and antiqued like the frame it was cut to fit even around the scrollwork. There were sixteen nails on the circumference of this backing, brass heads a little larger than a pin and, when I extracted them, no more than a quarter of an inch in length. Under that, a row of longer nails wedged a layer of thick card against the photograph and glass. These inner nails were so deeply rooted that some training in dentistry was wanted. I had to hold the frame between my knees, edge a screwdriver under the nail, grasp the head with the point of the pliers, and then wag it back and forth until the wood gave just enough to let me get a firmer grip for the extraction. It was clear that when Mr. Srofe went into this frame it was intended as an act of permanence, even immortality. Now it was Florida December, and I sweated a little before the last tooth came out.

It finally yielded to my pliers, and I lifted the glass and the portrait onto my palm.

Mr. Srofe was in his early forties, I'd guess, double-breasted dark suit buttoned across an upright slender torso. Both hands rested in the pockets, insouciant but not so deep as to disturb the horizontal slits. The thumbs hung forward, darkened to the first knuckle, so the broad nails stood out like pale extra buttons. Above the jacket a vest showing one more button trapped a wide tie with a pattern of interlocking leaves. The lapels were wide, the collar high. There was a handkerchief folded in the pocket — inexpertly, it seemed to me, but maybe the crush at the left, the point off-center, were part of a calculated casualness that I with my nineties sense of the casual could not interpret. This was a modern man, a man who made boxes as an art. He faced the camera directly with an enigmatic smile tucked between tall dimples. His head-on gaze was stern, the pinprick of shine that glanced off his pupils brighter than cardboard ought to be able to represent. He was set against the mottled backdrop that even today some operas — and Olan Mills — pretend for sky.

I slipped my new family — Kodachrome in gilt, a handsome pastiche — against the glass. Then I didn't know what to do with Mr. Srofe. With a slight sense of intimidation, I laid him behind Peter, Anne, and me, put back the cardboard and took up the first of the tiny nails.

I had a long time, fumbling with fingers too big and too big a hammer, to contemplate the point. It has got to be something about the impermanence of our postmodern lives, how restlessly we marry, frame, remarry, re-form, reframe.

But I was also keenly aware that the assumptions of Mr. Srofe's portrait were the ones I took to college with me in the middle of the fifties. When my Barnard class met on the occasion of our thirty-fifth reunion, we found ourselves in remarkable agreement about how we had charged around New York in stiletto heels and saddle shoes, knowing that we would marry, stay married, and raise families. Education was good for us; it would make us better mothers. Yet all of us remembered some incident of early rebellion, some surge of confused resentment at the way things were. In my case it was a play called *Garden Party* that I wrote on the impetus of anger at *Paradise Lost* and its macho-centric universe. The Eve I posited was a prelapsarian superwoman; she wanted babies, a bungalow in "Paradise Lots," to sculpt the Edenic mud, and as her dialogue keeps vaguely insisting, "to know."

What do we now know? Mine was the generation that cracked frames (in the current parlance, pushed the envelope). Standing to a certain extent on the shoulders of Srofe and ilk — packaging, repackaging, buying the disposable diapers and the flip-out frames, we stumbled our way toward our reconstituted families. The cost has been high — I too am worried about divorce and drugs and disaffection — but I hardly think society can recover its innocence by returning to the bootstrap ethic. Free enterprise has more to answer for than free love. We are for the most part more honest partners than our parents, and better parents. Second and surrogate families offer nests to thousands of us who would have been shoved to the margins in that more rigid generation. Mr. Srofe may have spent his artistic talent in industry; his daughter's, my stepmother's, was dismissed entirely.

One purpose of art has always been to hold a moment of fleeting time. Now surrounded with photographs and glass, I was reminded that picnickers of the eighteenth century used to pack a frame in the food basket and hold it up to help them "see" the view. This would amuse me more if Peter and I had not taken snapshots of our sunglasses in a dozen different landscapes. No doubt the need to hold and stay, the imperative of stillness, augments at the same pace as life. We have framed ourselves against the rocks off the Oregon coast, the flat glass of the Florida Atlantic, the onion towers of Budapest, the stone arches of Florence. We who are normally inventive take the same picture at every longitude, either or both of us at the lower left edge of a Wonder, as if to establish our sameness and permanence in a too-available world.

Frame of reference: a network of potential meaning within a given boundary. It occurs to me that each segment of a moving picture is called a frame, and that the cinema's obsession with mirrors, doors, and windows, which has lasted through its history and through styles as different as noir and European Art, is more than mere self-reflexivity and self-love. In a favorite shot, the camera pulls back from the mirror to reveal that we had misinterpreted by seeing only what was within the frame. "I was framed" means that the necessary truth of context was left out.

But a frame is also a celebration of category, a decoration for the way the human mind works, whose central business is to know this from that, to know where self ends and other begins, which are alien and which are kin. "Pigeonhole" is only "frame" in the pejorative.

I looked up from my task to the damp patches on the window; it was thirty degrees colder outside. I had a vivid memory of my mother opening the door to receive me when I fled my first marriage. Door, window, mirror: these framed flat spaces delineate essential categories: inside/outside, public/private, mine/yours, myself/the rest.

My hair frames my face. My picket fence frames my tended grass and flowers and separates them from the city's street; the ring road whirls traffic around the frame of our fair city, separating those who have business here from those who just want to pass on. We perceive a border carved by the sea around the continent, and add beach houses and marinas like scrollwork on a frame. The atmosphere frames the planet, and we fear the hole in the ozone less for the sake of melanoma than the threat of some essential edgelessness.

I'm not sentimental about Mr. Srofe and his bid for optic immortality. Those who supposed that photographs would be treasured like one-off oils were probably not thinking even as clearly as I am now; and in any case Srofe was a mover in the early boom of the throwaway culture and ought to have known better. We are all expendably packaged. A coffin is a frame to fix the last likeness. Alzheimer's is a form of biodegradation; and my unmet step-grandfather, who made cunning packages, was recyclable after all.

The new convolution of photographs is on the wall. Peter, Anne, and I grin from the center, the new nucleus of the new nuclear family, formed of fission and fusion, orbited by children, siblings, and progenitors alive and dead, strangers to each other, the fishmonger and the vintner grandfathers, the Hungarian exiles and the Irish immigrants. And Mr. Srofe is also there — his stiff lapel and his slouching handkerchief, his assumption of permanence and his niche in the culture of discard — concealed but palpable, pressing our noses to the glass.

Pool

Triple-A Experts says it can drop those two pines for six hundred dollars, sink the heads on a dime. They won't hurt the palm and they're not worried that the electric mains are in the way, though if I am worried the city will drop the line, too, temporarily, free of charge.

Skinny young Steve, one of the Triple A's, casts an expert glance at the base of a pine, implying the dime where the heads will fall, a hundred feet straight down. The spot is between the two azaleas, beside the rose and the nandina — which is to say, the exact spot where the preacher stood to marry my Dad to Gladys in 1976, the year the boys and I moved in, in what we had already taken to calling the Dog Yard though we did not yet have a dog. That day we put a satin bow on the gate, and Alex and Tim wore suits without a murmur. Dad and Gladys had driven all the way from Arizona. "Don't call it a dog yard," I said; "it's their wedding day!" — though I don't recall whether any of us slipped up. The boys are now in London and the Cameroons, respectively. Dad died in 1987 and Gladys is in a nursing home. The fourth of the dogs we didn't have yet is recuperating from allergies in Amherst, Mass.

The azaleas will survive a transplant, maybe; the rose maybe not; nandina, like flea eggs, can't be killed. I feel no guilt ecological or otherwise about the pines, because in this climate it's dogwood eat dogwood: red bud and magnolia spring up anywhere there's light. In 1985, Hurricane Kate tore out a couple of dozen trees, though it's not really something you can put a number to, because first you'd have to decide what constitutes a tree. There are volunteer water oaks and pecans no higher than the ivy, which probably won't make it in the fight for sun; there are weeds, up on a part of the hill too dense to climb, that are higher than my head and have six inches diameter of stem. I know people who would fell a sweet gum sooner than spit, and everybody talks "trash trees." In this town you don't need a permit to fell a pine unless it's four feet across.

City of Tallahassee will reroute the mains, but they will have to sink a pole, at a charge of nine hundred dollars. Clayton Spivey of Electric Power thinks we can get the line buried for not too much more, and he says to try Scarborough Electric.

John Scarborough, chewing a lip, lifting his cap to smooth his scalp, comes up with the notion that instead of hiring a trencher we could coordinate with the pool man's backhoe. He has priced out the rigid and the vinyl pipe, the 200-amp line, the new connection through the attic to the weatherhead. "And we have to give Mr. Peddie a little for the use of his tractor." It comes, after all, to about fourteen hundred dollars. "That's three hundred for me, to be frank with you, and that's not a lot."

I agree. But it's too much, and I'll have to go with the city's nine hundred dollar city pole. Mr. Scarborough doesn't mind. "Truth is, you get better conduction in the open air anyways."

"And the backhoe will tear up a lot of grass, wouldn't it?"

Mr. Scarborough chews on his grin. "Oh, grass. I can tell you your grass is going to be tore up. There's no way you'll not have to turf."

"I didn't think of that," I say. "What will that cost?"

Mr. Scarborough makes a soothing noise. "You don't have to do it all at once."

"I know, but maybe I'm getting in over my head."

He gestures at the base of the pine where the preacher stood, where the diving board will go. "That's the point, ain't it?"

I agree, laughing. "Is it worth it, do you think?"

"Oh, yes ma'am. I wouldn't do without my pool. I tell you, my missus has a little weight problem and I tend that way myself. But I get home, I do me a few curls and the both of us plunge in that water, it like to bring you back alive."

It occurs to me that I don't really know exactly what a "curl" is, though two images present themselves: the Shirley Temple ringlets I so badly wanted; and my dad's fleshy body rolling forward on the diving board, a thick arc from fingertips to splash in the brilliant water of the Encanto municipal swimming pool in Phoenix.

"Like to bring you back alive," Mr. Scarborough repeats, musing.
"Well, okay."

"Mr. Peddie will build you one beautiful hole."

Next morning the line is dropped and we have no power indoors,
but a raw sort of technology has taken over the street. A leather-faced
man all bone and sinew, with the pouched eyes of an alcoholic but the
reflexes of Mugsy Bogues, loops himself up one pine on a leather belt,
his chain saw dangling. The pine limbs come down neatly between azalea and rose, azalea and palm, and the head drops on a dime. Chain
buzz and pine smell wake the neighborhood. Thirty-foot sections of
trunk follow, shaking the earth till its teeth rattle. One section lands
perpendicular and gouges a foot deep (there's no way I'll not have to
turf), and then a plump black in a "Lifeguard" T-shirt circles the trunk
at ground level, slicing through the tree rings to the center.

The climber pauses between fellings for a cigarette. "I'm shaking,"
I say. "Is it still exciting for you?"

"It's a rush," he's pleased to admit. "My daddy said to me: 'You'll
never amount to anything, you won't stay in school, you don't care for
nothing but beer and girls, you better find something you like to do.'
So I did."

The second tree comes down, head falling toward me like a flower,
making tectonic thunder; a thirty-foot stem, another, and Lifeguard
circles the stump, sawing to the bull's-eye. They chop the trunks into
ten-foot logs; the black maw of the crane truck picks them up and
vomits them in the flatbed; and Triple-A Experts are outta here.

I love to watch competence, which gives me a sensation as close as I
come to patriotism. My dad was suspicious of my education, which
had too much "higher" in it, but he considered efficient maintenance
a virtue without gender. Therefore I clear my own drains and change
the seatings on the faucets; therefore also my sons can operate a sewing machine. Feminism can be husbanded and fathered as well as
mothered.

It is not twenty minutes before City of Tallahassee has arrived to
hook me up again. This time the pole climber is massive, with a curly
profusion of black hair and beard, but he nips nimbly up to the weatherhead. It occurs to me that I've cut down two live trees for six hundred dollars and intend to erect a dead one for another nine hundred.

"I've been trying to call Mr. Spivey," I say, "but he's not in the office today. I'll want you to sink that pole. It's too expensive to go underground."

Blackbeard makes a sympathetic face. "It's awful, ain't it."

"I've wanted a pool in this spot since '76," I defend myself. "But I thought it would be about what I had to spend, and it's nowhere near. I'll be going in debt again." I am apologizing partly because this man reminds me of my dad, who had his girth but not his hair, and was a competent workman who would have loved to own a swimming pool but would never have borrowed for such an extravagance.

Blackbeard pinches the sweat from his beard. He has picked up on the apologizing, because he says, no irony, "Well, you got to have your pool! It's the way we live."

The machine is in the garden. The dozer end of the backhoe has skimmed off the ivy, poison and benign, like the scum on stew, and Mr. Peddie's layout man has chalked out a shape on the ground. The shape is called a balanced kidney, which sounds medically impeccable. A burned and muscled shirtless man chops the chalk line with an axe. Now the rear end of the hoe plants itself on its mantis legs, sets its teeth in the axe's groove, bites and spits huge mouthsful of the rich mix of roots and earth. Three more burned and muscled shirtless men follow the perimeter with sharp shovels, slicing a perfect perpendicular.

Clayton Spivey has also arrived and planted a stake in the heart of the trash pile, tied a red rag on it. Mr. Spivey has a very short gray crew cut, a jogging jacket in spite of the heat, a fastidious air. He seems rather disappointed that I've decided against the buried line. "Aesthetically, of course, it'd be preferable."

"I know. But I picked the best pool, and anything else will have to be done bit by bit."

"Is it very expensive, putting in a pool?" he asks.

"Very."

"But you have the perfect spot for it."

How kindly everyone reassures me! Mr. Spivey sits in his truck to write the details of the estimate. Mr. Peddie is back to check on the progress and make sure the hole is going where I want it. Mr. Peddie is in his late fifties, very tall and very slender, speaks softly, moves gently; the crease in the short sleeve of his plaid shirt looks as if it was ironed half an hour ago. He talks swim-out and sand filter, skimmers and pump, in no hurry, though these are things we have already discussed, making sure I am sure of my decisions. He shows me the tile edging in several shades of plain blue, a stylized wave, and a symmetrical Florentine-looking medallion. I pick this last without hesitation, and Mr. Peddie tells me it's surely the prettiest. It occurs to me that he would say this no matter what I'd picked, but I have by now such faith in his honesty that I dismiss the thought as small-minded.

Until nearly noon the pool site was in shade from the pines and oaks across the street, but now the sun is full and blistering where the hoe chomps and the men slice with their shovels. The straight sides show a foot or so of brown-black topsoil; below that the dirt is as red as hair. In spite of the wet air and the lush growth, this iron earth is as dry as Arizona sand. Roots protrude from it like whiskers, resilient and tough. The men patiently shave them with their pointed spades. At one point the backhoe hits concrete; the driver hacks at it again and again with the grating racket of metal on cement. It's an old septic tank, they think, from before this land was part of the city. It doesn't trouble them, they'll break through what they need to break through, leave the rest. Mr. Peddie suggests that there may have been a house on this lot once.

The image that has hung around my mind all morning comes to the foreground: Dad staking and stringing for the foundation of an Arizona bungalow, digging a deep rectangle to pour the concrete that will support a structure the hollow obverse of this one. I lean over the red hole with a touch of vertigo, and I realize that I am in the process of doing something odd, gouging out a place to hold more water in this water-laden climate.

Mr. Spivey, leaving, tells us sadly about a woman the city did some electrical work for, who owns a piece of land pretty as this one. Her husband died and her son moved away, she paid for dirt, had it hauled in, and filled in her swimming pool.

"Can you believe that?"

I can believe it. I look at the hole, three-quarters dug in half a day, and at the man in the cockpit who with his levers makes the backhoe bite into the pool's south wall. He snags roots the size of my arm, dumps them on the spot where the preacher stood, where the diving board will go. I can imagine being old, alone, finding the pine needles and the loss too much to handle.

But not now. Now I sit on the stump of the pine and see my chunk of Florida from under a canopy translucent with the sky behind. One of the men aims his spade at a stubborn tentacle of one of the felled pines and wrenches it out of the red wall. The first of our four dogs is buried up on the other side of the fence; this side, one of his ham bones is tossed up by the back hoe.

Where we dig and what we build describes our passing. My dad loved the water but settled in the desert, a small contractor who could pour a fine foundation, but never had a pool. When the boys were seven and ten I didn't have the option of giving them this extravagance. Now it will be my stepdaughter whose childhood passes here. The dogs and the excavated septic tank yield their place to my eventual grandchildren. I imagine a collar of roses around the deck, a bed of impatiens, a plot of summer tulips.

PC and PC

" was so glad to quit writing," says Gary, who has come to install the fax. Gary is a strange fellow for a hacker: he's made his living as a freelance journalist and as a talk show host; his mother tongue seems to be standard English, not cyberspeak; he agrees with me that I probably don't need the Net, and his instructions for the PC seem generally designed to enable me to make it do what I need instead of impressing me with what it, or he, can do.

I've asked, "Is it okay, doing computers for a living?" and he replies, "Oh, yeah, I was *so* glad to quit writing, it's just fine."

It's true, writing is harder than most people think. I say something of the sort. But it isn't that. Gary tells me about going on assignment to Peru. He was supposed to trace the footsteps of a Florida reporter who had been murdered under ambiguous circumstances. He thinks he figured out what happened. But there was, he says, no way he could write about Peru.

"I saw people with carts selling used baggies. I saw a knife fight over a refrigerator carton, to use as a shelter. I had never understood that trash is a luxury." But, he says, he also realized there was no way to write about such poverty without appearing to celebrate by contrast our superior lifestyle. To write about it in the glossy magazine that had given him the assignment in the first place was to take part in the corporate world that generates our trash.

While I am pondering this, it comes to me that I've never written a word about India.

"Lucky you," said about half my friends when I told them, in 1984, that I was going to India. The other half produced physical signs of aversion — a wrinkled nose, raised eyebrow, fending-off gesture: "Why would you want to look at all that poverty?"

I thought that missed the point, but when I got to Delhi I realized that I had missed it, too. My experience of India was intensely and awkwardly egotistical, self-centered in the way that I have experienced depression, as a trap of self. Too tall, too pasty-pale, sweating, showing too much arm, I had no right way to be. I was by definition rich, since I could afford to have traveled there. If I ignored or refused the child who dogged my footsteps, I felt simultaneously haughty and gangly, askew to my identity. If I gave in and handed the child a few rupees I was instantly conspicuous for the wake I drew of other beggars. If I bought the mirror-embroidered skirt for ten dollars, I fostered an industry in which the woman who embroidered it made about ten cents a day. If I didn't buy it she was out ten cents.

My host, Blair Kling, was a Caucasian American scholar of Indian history who has lived off and on for thirty years in Delhi, Calcutta, and Bombay; and who is considered by other scholars to write from a straddle-perspective, as Indian as Western even when he is not writing about India. His position on the beggars was unequivocal, perhaps less like a resident alien than like an Indian of higher caste. He ignored them and instructed me to ignore them; at most he gestured lightly away. He knew that he made his contribution in the universities, his sacrifices in the temples; he "knew his place," you might say, and was at ease in it.

I could not be so. I smiled insincerely, averted my eyes still less sincerely, angry with India and ashamed for myself fifty times a day in minute ways.

But even he was sometimes caught. We arrived in Agra by hired car, five hours of 110-degree heat from Delhi: Blair, his wife Julia, who is my closest friend, their daughter Joanna, and I. As soon as we alighted we were claimed by a boy of about ten with the usual frayed shirt, bare feet, the usual enormous eyes. He pressed a brochure on us and offered to be our guide.

"No, it's all right," said Blair. "I know the Taj Mahal very well; we won't need a guide." But the boy stuck to us while we toured, Blair giving us the history, the myth, the architectural details. Each time he came to the end of a paragraph the boy thrust forward his brochure and said, "I guide." We were hot and tired. Blair explained that he *was* a guide, that we thanked him very much but we would like to tour on our own. It went on for about an hour. Finally, irritated, Blair reached in his pocket and thrust forward a handful of rupees.

The boy's face blanched and he drew himself up, four feet of dignity, batting the bills away. "I am a *guide*," he said fiercely, meaning: not a beggar. And for the rest of the afternoon he stayed beside us, not speaking another word, while we admired the cool marble caverns of that monument to love, sick with the insult we had given.

Looking at is the right concept for a tourist in India. All the senses are by turns assaulted, alerted, bathed; but sight is what I remember, the knife-edge meeting of flat brown earth and flat blue sky, along which some flash of impossible color appears on sari or camel blanket or vendor's cart: cerise or citron, magenta, turquoise, purple, cerulean, gold. Peacocks in the grounds of the Rambagh Palace thundered their tails at monkeys the color of buttered toast. I can see the cut gemstones tumbling in Dixie cups under a striped awning in Jaipur — aquamarine, ruby, emerald, garnet, pearl. I can see the pale palms of children held at the height of my elbow, an alien patience, lined with grime.

In my few weeks there I managed one subversive act. We went several times to the Hanuman Temple with an Indian colleague who had pledged a series of sacrifices to the god. Outside this temple there sat day after day a slender (emaciated?) woman of perhaps thirty, whose two children played quietly (listlessly?) nearby. Each time we passed she rolled her hand gently from the wrist, less like a supplication than like a gesture from ballet. I have, notice, no way to say this without a Western reference, so that I feel now something of the out-of-kilter awkwardness I felt as I walked past her. But one day my friends had gone on a little ahead of me, and I put a hand in my pocket and lay my finger against my lips as I slipped the money to her. She nodded, pocketed the bills, put her palms together in the gesture of blessing, and, bowing just slightly over her hands, flashed me a smile of mischievous understanding. After that, every time I passed her I was ready with a palmed bill, she was ready to sleight-of-hand it, and from a distance we would bow to each other, conspirators.

"Are there nuances of bigotry?" — the interviewer asked my opinion. Oh, my, yes, there are nothing but nuances. Bigotry comes in nuances the way sand comes in grains. Get your feet wet and you'll be carrying them into the car, sifting them into the corners of your fancy condo. What I have done to or with or around this image of the bowing woman is to "romanticize" or "sentimentalize" it, central sins in the canon of hegemony. I also, however, romanticize and sentimentalize my marriage, my children, my friendships, and many aspects of my profession, and far from being a sin this seems to be a source of community and mutual joy. Julia and I tell the story of our inauspicious meeting in Binghamton, New York, to anyone who will listen. Peter and I celebrate our anniversaries telling each other over candlelight our history thus far.

Perhaps it is all right to romanticize a relationship as long as both partners do so equally; only when one romanticizes from the position of oppressor is the sweetness false? I'm happy with this for a minute, but then realize that in many oppressive relationships romanticization is both a form of denial and a survival technique. Women in abusive marriages, for example, help to trap themselves this way — and indeed I have used sentimentality as a form of inertia in more than one impossible situation.

"Some of my best friends are Jews," my mother said, and looking back on it, I assess that she had very few friends, and that two of them were Jews. I was into my twenties before I caught on that this was a self-betraying thing to say — maybe my first PC moment — and it took much longer to pin down exactly why it wouldn't do. Now one of my students strugglingly writes, "The black people I have met since then have not seemed any different to me than any people I have ever met," and this self-deconstructing sentence demonstrates the problem nicely. "Black people" are set in opposition to "any people"; therefore by definition the category of "any people" does not include black people, and to deny that they "seemed any different" is not a semantic possibility.

But to suppose that these difficulties of the language do not need respectful address is to perpetuate a further bigotry against those whose "consciousnesses" have had no chance for loft. My mother spent four years, from the ages of five to nine, in an isolated marble quarry in the Chiricahua Mountains of southern Arizona. Her father was the manager of a crew of Mexicans, who had perhaps a dozen or twenty children with whom she was not allowed to play. She sat alone on a rock that she called her best friend and watched them, for four years. Did she grow up believing that Mexicans were untouchables? How could she have borne her life if she had not? Later she taught me to box up the old toys at Christmas and take them "south of the tracks." What is the difference between those secondhand teddy bears and the weathered rupees in my palm? Nuance and nuance. Sand and sand.

"Do you have someone to clean your house for you?" the interviewer asked Jamaica Kincaid on NPR. Yes, said Ms. Kincaid. How did she feel about that? Well, she said, it was an exchange of money for work, an honorable exchange, it did not require *love*, though she herself, as a young immigrant maid in New York, had been loved. . . . The exchange dwindled mawkishly.

And it was a relief to know that the Cinderella of belles lettres, who also sees colonialism with such fierce clarity, deals with the issue as gingerly as I. The truth is that we all live in bad faith. As we maneuver the global shrinkage, across race, class, caste, and cultures, we are all tourists in India, intensely self-conscious, politically correct as a further form of sentimentality because, really, we have no right way to be. To espouse political correctness is to impose another artificial order (like law, religion, borders, quotas, myth) on a pervasive mess. The best thing I have been able to recognize, to do, is to continue to "raise my consciousness," which means to become ever more aware of these grating bits of tenacious grit, buying care at the perpetual cost of spontaneity.

Bessie Anthony and I negotiate the mined ground carefully. We are not from alien countries; we pay our taxes to the same assessor, take our drivers' tests out of the same shed. Nevertheless — she has cleaned my house four hours a week since 1978 — received icons lie in wait for us. She asked me once if I was familiar with the TV show *Hazel*. "That was always the way I saw myself," she said wistfully, and of course she didn't mean she wanted to be white like the old sitcom housekeeper, but that she had wanted one full-time employer to whom she was necessary, by whom loved. We trip and fall into other clichés. I can think of Bessie as a treasure, as part of the family. She can boss me like a mammy.

But we manage, mainly by mutual romanticizing of our peculiar history, exactly as I do with Julia, with my brother, husband, kids. Bessie and I have been into and out of alcohol together, have seen each other through divorce. Our children have been in and out of the army, in and out of love. Her grandson married an Italian, my son is in love with a Punjabi Sikh. Our progeny have inhabited half a dozen countries among them, one of hers in Germany, one of mine in Africa, negotiating the shrinking ground. We are harsh on each other's past men, celebratory and congratulatory on each of us having found, her singlehood, my husband. I am short of time and she of money, so when she knows I'm under pressure she stays an extra hour to clean the cupboards, put this or that in order; when I know her car is in the shop or the family coming in for the weekend I double her pay. We can ask for help but are more likely to be anticipated; we thank with a hug, send notes naming each other as good friends. She praises my Peter by telling me I am happy, in a stance of mock-protectiveness ("You tell him: I'm booking it down"). I irritate her by letting things get to me, she irritates me by recommending Jesus. It isn't perfect but it stands my test of friendship, which only a few of my friendships do: what would it take, to get me to walk out of Bessie's life, she out of mine? Answer: it can't be done.

But this ease does not permeate certain social boundaries, most of them determined by gender. When I pay Gary to install my modem or my new program, it is an untainted exchange. No threat of inequality comes between us; whereas because Bessie changes the sheets and cleans the stove, that threat must be fought off day by day — there's something here not about race or class but about the value of women's work. On the other hand, she and I can sit down to chat over coffee with her sister but not her brother, with my women but not my men colleagues. Perhaps these same men can leap the barriers of money and status with their mechanics or in sports bars? I have never been invited to Bessie's house, and the twice she came with her boyfriend to my parties we both felt awkward, and let that go. I think I would argue that these social convolutions are not more complex than others I maneuver through and around and in — the A's are invited to large parties but not to dinner with the B's; Aunt C. will come to dinner at home but hates restaurants — but these particular convolutions pulse with the special soreness of race and class.

My grad student Val says, "I have my ideologies, and then I have my life. I know that."

My modem is up and running, but I'm not ready for the Net. I sit here walking this fine line with the boy in Agra, the woman at the temple, Bessie. Strugglingly, making sentences out of Blair's inconsistencies, Gary's, my mother's, Bessie's, Kincaid's, mine.

Val says, "Gary's a hoot. He's gonna avoid the corporate world by installing computers? Get real. Anyway, you believe he isn't writing? Not me, not for a second."

We Eat the Earth

or six years in the sixties I was tenant of an English garden. Oh, my name was on the mortgage. I had come from as far away as an Arizona childhood to teach English at the University of Sussex, where my Belgian husband would direct the Gardner Centre for the Arts. We had bought, for what was then about thirty-four thousand dollars — more than we could afford — a bleak brick box on two acres of rolling land under the South Downs. The house had big cube rooms smudged ochre with twenty years of ash, and many mullioned window panes of which one hundred eight were broken. But these windows looked onto a garden that had been tended for thirty years by the man who had designed it so that no prospect would ever be free of flowers and it would yield food in every month. South, a gravel drive, a stand of bamboo and flowering cherry; west and north, lawns reaching to the ruin of a tennis court, lush rose beds, and an orchard; and east to a greenhouse, more orchard, and a rectangle of about two-thirds of an acre *laid to* (as I learned to say) vegetables and fruit. You could see from this garden no other house, only fields cropped short by sheep and cows, sloping gently away or, beyond the road, rising to the crest of the Downs.

We could not really afford a gardener, but we could rent out the "staff flat" to graduate students, and the rent would pay for two and a half days a week of Mr. Ashley's time. Mr. Ashley said that he could find someone to hire him the other three days (we learned only gradually what an understatement this was), and so it was arranged. We told him to simplify in whatever way he needed to, in order to keep the garden in less than half the usual time. He said he would like a power hedge clipper and to eliminate one twenty-foot bed of dahlias. We said fine.

I was seven months pregnant when we moved in; we had a toddler and two jobs. We set frantically to work with white paint on the ceilings and a sander on the crumbling-varnish floors. Mr. Ashley freewheeled down the gravel in the early mornings in a peaked cap and a three-piece suit of hard tweed with a fob across the vest. He was white haired, blue eyed, trim, and soft-spoken. He never hurried but was seldom still. Invited inside, he demurred shyly. Invited to bring his wife to dinner, he declined embarrassed. He would not take a cup of tea. He called my husband "The Governor" and me "The Missus."

In the third or fourth week, toward the end of September, he brought us a seed catalog and asked what we would like him to grow in the way of fruits and vegetables. We read through it uneasy at our ignorance. We had no idea what could be grown in this soil or climate, or what would need too much care for two-and-a-half-days a week. After a while I took the catalog back outside and explained to Mr. Ashley that we had simply checked everything that, if he grew it, we would eat. "You decide whatever is convenient."

In an hour or so he was back at the back door. "Melons," he said hesitantly, "require daily care."

"Oh," I said. "Fine."

He fingered deliberately the pages of the catalog.

"Otherwise that'll be all right."

And it was. In the greenhouse tomatoes climbed and blazoned out of herbal beds; Belgian endive thickened its pallor inside upended terra-cotta pots. Cucumber vines tickled their way through seedling lettuce and early radishes in the hothouse frames. Every year there were two sorts each of green beans, onions, spinach, peas (petits first and then English), cabbage, and carrots. There were garlic, scallions, turnips, cauliflower, beets, broccoli, brussels sprouts, kale, catnip, asparagus. We helped bag the potatoes and box the apples that lasted through the winter. Mr. Ashley braided the onions and the garlic. I went to school to the garden, and I learned (ignorant child of Arizona!) that that black slash on a potato is the wound of a pitchfork. I learned how to put my foot on the edge of a spade, drive it straight so as not to hit the side of a leek, pull straight up, slice off the tops, and make vichyssoise (which the boys learned to call swishy-swodge). I canned peas. I put up a hundred pints of jam — strawberry, loganberry, gooseberry, red currant and black currant. We bought a freezer, and I learned how to lay raspberries on a cookie sheet and bag them hard as marbles. I stewed and froze tomatoes. I scalloped and froze potatoes. We got a dog and cats, then rabbits and a goat. The dog and cats ate table scrap and the rabbits and goats digested the peels and husks of Mr. Ashley's bounty. I tried making elderberry wine (not much good). I made rhubarb tarts (superb). I dug and grated fresh horseradish. I dried mushrooms from the cow-rich field next door.

I have no vocabulary for those tastes. "Vine-ripened" is merest adspeak for a tomato's seeded juice, warm as the palm of a hand. A carrot resists your tug, hugging the spring earth, and breaks sweet under grit. A bean snaps sharp on the teeth but asparagus yields with a soft *thock*. A potato just dug and boiled has the texture of hot snow. The half of the apple that hasn't rotted on the ground bites back with a tartness just this side of wine. Once a Belgian visitor to whom I served Stew Gaston cried, "*On mange de la terre ici!*" and I thought: we eat from the earth, but the other translation feels also true: we eat the earth.

Not everything I learned had to do with food, of course. I learned how to stand white-knuckled at the sink letting the boys climb sixty feet into the horse chestnut tree, and then how to thread the chestnuts so they could have conker wars. I learned how to gather a couple of hundred daffodils from the orchard in such a way that you couldn't tell I'd been there, how to cut roses on the diagonal an inch above the lowest five-leaf branch, how to balance a trug on my forearm and scrape the mud from my Wellingtons.

I never wanted to leave that garden, and remembering it makes the shape of the word *yearn* in my throat. From time to time I would dream I was walking down the lawn, which was full of fine ladies in cartwheel hats, trying to convince them that it had once been mine. I frequently performed little rituals of ownership, taking the children along the concrete paths that crossed the vegetable beds, counting the rose bushes, smelling the apple trees, tugging gingerly on the head of a raspberry but pinching thumbnail-onto-finger through the stem of a gooseberry. I became adept at seeing the camouflaged buds of peony and laburnum in midwinter. I made a sweet infusion of the first golden raspberry leaves. In difficult times, and there were difficult times in the six years I was there, I sat at the bottom of the vegetable plot with my back to the loganberry trellis, gazing at the Downs and chanting under my breath "I lift up mine eyes unto the hills."

But though I had registered for the long term, the garden never belonged to me. For someone born into the desert and the world of the typewriter, that plot of fecund soil was akin to a computer — in that it could do far more than I could take in or master. I surfed the legumes and the roots, making demands to which they mysteriously complied, but I was barely literate in their mysteries. Mr. Ashley never to my knowledge tasted anything from "our" rich patch — he had his own smaller garden. Every year we entered his zucchini, his runner beans, his peonies and irises in the Westmeston Flower Show, and (to his pride) carried home his prizes. Even the three-toed carrot with which Tim, seven, won the Weird Vegetable ribbon, was properly speaking Mr. Ashley's deformity.

We struggled with the house, the children, the university, a theater, each other. Mr. Ashley wheeled down the gravel in every weather, sat in the wet in the shed sharpening his tools or braiding onions. When the weather broke he was out again in his tweed vest and trousers, packing straw under the berries (ignorant Arizonan! — so that's where they got their name), tying up the runner beans, bending little houses of chicken wire over the seedling peas to thwart the field mice. Mr. Ashley was never absent. He was never hurried. Nothing in the garden ever failed to sprout or fruit. Once we wheeled him into a vacation, and he went with his wife to his brother's for a week — where, Mrs. Ashley said, he sat and wrung his hands wanting to get back to "our" raspberries and beets. I loved the garden in bursts of energy and emotion, but I came to understand that Mr. Ashley had the nature for a garden. I did not. I was impetuous and rash. Invention was my virtue, and enthusiasm. Steady growing wants a steady guide, wants calm and continuity, almost submission.

I had no obligation but to consume. Even so, the garden's demands became heavier, or I became less capable of meeting them. We were living in several ways beyond our means. There were weekends when we sent visitors away with armloads of squash and fennel and cabbage — but could not stand a round of drinks at the local pub. Sometimes when we came home at midnight from the Gardner Centre for the Arts, weary with imminent production, Mr. Ashley would have left word that the peas were ready; and I would go into the garden with a flashlight to pick them, would stay up all night canning or freezing. How could I let them go to waste? When the production was over, I would cook for cast parties, thick soups and mountains of sliced vegetables and berry parfaits. How could I not share such readily available wealth? I flung tops and stalks to the goat, who became unaccountably bad-tempered, and then threatening. I washed rivers of mud down the sink until the septic tank backed up.

In 1971 I left my husband, left England, left the garden. I took the boys, their toys, a suitcase apiece of essential clothes, and headed back to America with very little notion of what I was doing except that I had been living in more than one way beyond my means. At Gatwick Airport I folded my keys into an envelope addressed back to the Sussex house, and dropped the envelope in the postbox. It was a chilly December dawn. When I crossed to the plane, a child on each hand, I had in my field of vision the black expanse of the tarmac, and suddenly superimposed on it the rows of turnip tops, the beans on their stakes, the rush of roses, the apple trees bending below the grassy hump of the down. I was doing the right thing, I knew even then, and for that sick and stunning moment knew even then, that I would never be done with grieving for the garden.

I still make Stew Gaston and, peeling the potatoes for it, hope to find the verifying black wound of somebody's pitchfork. I still make vichyssoise, from leeks I buy three at a time, a dollar apiece, at Publix. The boys, now thirty-one and thirty-three, still call it swishy-swodge.

Of the Beholder

"'ll see it when I believe it," said some astute and bitter wag of the Rodney King tapes.

And it occurred to me that the moment of this shift, from *seeing is believing* to *believing is seeing*, represents the fulcrum between the scientific and the postmodern ethos. Ever since we have been climbing out of the muck of the dark ages, relying ever more on verifiable evidence and calculation, we have referred ourselves to clear sight and enlightenment. Now chaos theory and critical theory, the Heisenberg principle, second and third thoughts about Orientalism and the supposed westward-headed history of this continent — these and a hundred other small and large holes in our hope of progress — suggest to us that clear sight is an illusion, perspective is all, and that all of us are bigoted willy-nilly by our vantage point. Science, it turns out, is another metaphor, having more to do with the way the brain works than the way the world does.

Never mind; I'll tell a story about our cat.

Peter and I had each of us separately agreed never to pay money for a feline, and we agreed on it together. But we needed a replacement for a dear departed calico; it was Christmas, and free kittens were scarce; this litter was recommended to us by a friend, and we made the usual mistake of taking seven-year-old Anne along for a look.

We named her Paprikash for too little reason to recount. She was a silver Persian out of the picture books, blue eyes in a fur muff, born proud and sexy. She had her own sense of kitsch, choosing baskets out of which to drape a paw, making pedestals for self-display equally out of a computer, a pile of laundry, a bookshelf, and a dinner plate. As she grew she developed wiles and a certain, well, cattiness. She would stand in front of me at dinner time kneading the rug at my feet, soundless, blinking soulful. But when the food came down she dealt with neutered Cheddar and spayed Madeleine with swift scratches to the nose, perfunctory, like a queen with divine right and a quick temper.

I had thought that females didn't wander, but Paprikash was a slut. She would ooze against my leg to be let out. She would scratch out a screen if I refused, howl for the street, take off at night, and come back batting her albino lashes at dawn. She would roll her body like Betty Boop, push her gorgeous hair behind her ear.

No one had ever, in my experience, returned a cat to its owner, but neighbors and strangers would appear at the door, Paprikash cradled against a breast or draped over a hand, slightly accusatory, "Is this your cat? She's so *beautiful*." Twenty or thirty times I tried to suggest that even beautiful cats like the outdoors and can't be fenced in like dogs, but I don't think I ever convinced anyone. I was clearly cold at heart if my ball of silver fluff was up a dogwood.

More surprising than her wandering was Paprikash's prowess as a mouser. Preening to cover her stalking, padding delicately over the ivy, turning a dumb-blond stare — she rid the woods of a couple hundred shrews in her first year, flung snakes in our laps, dug frogs out of the skimmer, and once, all teenage bounce and bobby sox, sunk her fangs in the neck of a poisonous skink that Peter had to finish off with a machete.

Here's the thing. She was so gorgeous, so sought after and desired by other folk who admired cats, that we'd've liked to let her have a litter of her own, but there was some arcane rule in the kitty register, less to do with pet population than with diluting the breed, I think, and so when she was not quite a year old I made an appointment to have her spayed.

It was the night before the appointment, coincidentally, that I picked her up at an unusual angle and felt, through the thick fur — the Princess and the Pea comes to mind — two tiny balls.

"Peter? Look."

"Nah. That's vulva, got to be."

But it wasn't, and next morning Paprikash was fixed instead of spayed.

When he came home he was utterly changed. It wasn't a question of neutering but the opposite. All those slithers and wiles had become palpably masculine. The white ruff was leonine — why hadn't I seen it?— and the kneading of paws an understated Godfather threat. He was a natural hunter, slayer of reptiles and the varmints who excavated underground; a neighborhood lothario, prowler after pussy. Of course he had patriarchal rights to the food dish, and if he sought pedestals for self-display, it was in the manner of a monarch, not a girl. His very preening was a form of intimidation.

Eventually Paprikash ran away or was stolen — the latter more likely, I think, given his propensity and that of the passersby; he may be far away or, for all I know, immured behind one of the windows down the street — and was replaced by Chelsea, who was free, alley variety, and anatomically female. Chelsea is a stay-at-home and a silly-putty lover of people, but as fierce as Paprikash when it comes to food, of either the canned or the critter sort. Sometimes, knowing what I know, I try to imagine that she's a he and see if it changes my view of these inconsistencies. But although it is my profession so to imagine, and I have turned myself mentally into many a male character, it doesn't work. I "know what I know," and Chelsea stays stubbornly cute.

It's not that I reject the notion of clues to gender, age, race, ethnicity, or sexual proclivity. On the contrary (I hold forth to my writing students), details that delineate the individual also announce a "type," largely because we ourselves accept and don behaviors, clothes, patterns of speech as markers of our identity and belonging. "Political correctness" is the butt of many a snigger because, in order to condemn blanket judgments, the PC police deny the information in legitimate signs. But the reverse leads unto error: when we jump to an assumption, we misread the clues and read clues that are not *there*.

For instance:

1. In a famous anthropology case, the daily face-scarification ritual of the males of the Nacirema tribe is described. It is clear that status is conferred by the regular morning application of a knife or knives to the mandible; but the significance of this practice is not well understood. Probably it is a test of manliness through the withstanding of pain. (*Nacirema* is *American* spelled backward.)

2. Karen took the train to meet her lover in Nottingham. He drove to meet her at the station. He is a handsome Sierra Leonean airline pi-

lot. She found him rigid with restrained rage. He said, "I am leaning on the elbow of my sixty-pound Armani shirt on the roof of my BMW, and five people have asked me if I'm a taxi."

3. My friends Toby and Trish are attempting a nonsexist education for ten-month-old Katharine. For that reason, and because they're grateful for any sort of hand-me-down, they dress her sometimes in a frock, sometimes in T-shirt and trousers. Toby tells me that not only do people assume her gender from her clothes, not only assign her characteristics to fit the assumption, but if they think she's a boy they direct their praise to the parents — "Ooo, he's a strapping fellow, isn't he?" — and if a girl, to the child — "Aren't you the pretty, then?" This is a fine example of cultural self-fulfilling prophecy, handing on the lesson that girls may be engaged in immediate relationship whereas boys have to be dealt with on the oblique. Lexical note: *To strap* means "to secure something, to bind up" (as a wound), and "to beat with a strap." Which of these last three most likely led to the definition of *strapping* as "big, strong, sturdy in build," hmmm? In fact, Katharine is both pretty and strapping.

"Beauty is in the eye of the beholder," my mother used to say with a pious air, but I knew she meant that there was no accounting for Mr. Jones's uxorious treatment of Mrs. Jones, or Ms. Smith's strange predilection for young Thomson. Much more astute, and of a breathtaking daring, was her treatment of one six-year-old who came to her for speech lessons. This boy's mother had called distraught; her son had been stuttering ever since he started school. She was at her wits' end. Could my mother help? They made an appointment, and the doorbell rang at the specified time. My mother opened the door to discover a head of golden shoulder-length ringlets above a murderous scowl. She cordially told the woman to come back in half an hour, took the boy into the bathroom, and cut his hair. It is family lore that the cure was affected on the spot.

In recounting these latter episodes I get to be the good guy. I know the anthropology trick, I empathize with the African, I'm the liberal-hearted friend: therefore I commiserate and shake my head at the dimwittedness of the populace. In the more complicated signals my mother sent, I can observe both her guts and her sin of self-certainty. But if the gender of a kitten can lead me into serious and convoluted error, how much complacency may I be allowed? Crusader against sexism, racism, agism, and homophobia, just when I expect it least my own presumptions bang me on the forehead crude as a stepped-on rake — to remind me that, like learning itself, like spiritual quest, like recovery from psychopathology, *gaining perspective* is a process never finished.

Soldier Son

I had been to a couple of parties here before — a slightly stuffy, pleasantly scruffy London flat with worn leather on the chairs, Kurdish rugs on the floor, and etchings of worthy ruins on the walls. It looked like a grown-up version of Cambridge "digs," and most of us looked like middle-aged versions of the Cambridge undergraduates we had mostly been — now pundits and publishers, writers and actors, what the British call the "chattering classes." Both my sons were with me on this trip, sixteen-year-old Alex out with his guitar and the punks of Piccadilly Circus, nineteen-year-old Tim somewhere in the adjoining room in Harris tweed. I recognized the man crossing toward me glass-in-hand as somebody I vaguely knew — first name Jeff (or Geoff), last name lost. Slender, sandy, he looked too young to be the president of London P.E.N. International, though I seemed to remember that's what he was. I remembered he was witty and articulate, an impassioned campaigner for free speech and the freeing of imprisoned writers — my kind of person. So I was glad to see him headed toward me.

He charged a little purposefully though, his look a little heated. "I've been talking to your son," he said, and set his glass against his chin. "My God, how do you stand it?!"

My stomach clenched around its undigested canapés, brain wrung like a sponge. Shame, defensiveness, and rage (*I am responsible for my son; I am not responsible for my son; who are you to insult my son?*) so filled my throat that I could not immediately speak. What I felt was that I, literally, closed down. The free-speech champion offered me the kind of face, sympathy and shock compounded, that one offers to the victim of mortal news.

"I manage," I managed presently, and turned on my heel.

I have never so far as I know run into Jeff or Geoff again, but I credit him with the defining moment, when choice is made at depth: the Mother Moment.

Let's be clear. I live in knee-jerk land, impulses pacifist to liberal, religion somewhere between atheist and ecumenical, inclined to quibble and hairsplit with my friends, who however are all Democrats and Labour, ironists, believe that sexual orientation is nobody's business, that intolerance is the world's scourge, that corporate power is a global danger, that war is always cruel and almost always pointless — that guns kill people.

My son Tim, who describes himself as a fiscal conservative and social liberal, shares these attitudes of tolerance with regard to sex, race, and religion. His politics, however, emanate from a spirit of gravity rather than irony. Now thirty-three, he is a member of the Young Republicans, the National Rifle Association, and the United States Army Reserve, with which he spends as much time as he can wangle, most recently in Bosnia, Germany, and the Central African Republic, all places where, he says, he felt that he was "making a difference," "doing something that mattered" — also, "on the tip of the spear."

I love this young man deeply, and deeply admire about three-quarters of his qualities. For the rest — well, Jungian philosopher James Hillman has somewhere acknowledged those parts of every life that you can't fix, can't escape, and can't reconcile yourself to. How you manage those parts he doesn't say. What Tim and I do is let slide, laugh, mark a boundary with the smallest frown or gesture, back off, embrace, or shrug. Certainly we deny. Often we are rueful. I don't think there is ever any doubt about the "we."

Most parents must sooner or later, more or less explicitly, face this paradox: If I had an identikit to construct a child, is this the child I'd make? No, no way. Would I trade this child for that one? No, no way.

This week in Florida I receive in the mail a flyer from Teddy Kennedy that asks me to put my money where my mouth is, and my mouth is by fund-raising ventriloquism assumed to be saying, "Yes! I will stand up and be counted to help end the gun violence that plagues our country." I am considering a contribution when Tim drops by. Recently returned from nine months in Frankfurt with SOCEUR (Special Operations Command Europe), this afternoon he is headed *back* to the gun show where he spent an earlier hour, thinking he will maybe indulge himself to a Ruger because it's a good price, has a lovely piece of cherry on the handle and fine scoring, and he's never *had* a cowboy-type gun. He's curious how it handles, heavy as it is. And a single-action will be new to him. Later still he comes back by to show it off. He fingers the wood grain and the metal work, displays the bluing on the trigger mechanism — exactly as I would show off the weave of a Galway tweed, the draping quality of this crepe cut on the bias. He offers it on the palms of both hands, and I weigh it on mine, gingerly. "It's neat," I admit. Grinning at my caution he takes it back.

I used to say I don't know where he came from. I remember in the late sixties, when he was a toddler, standing in a gloriously sunlit kitchen laughing to a friend: "I don't mind gay, and I think I could handle drugs, or even prison. Just please don't let him come home a priest!" — his father had had a teenage flirtation with the Catholic Church. In the event, Tim spent a few years as an Episcopal, a mainly social interest as he admitted at the time, then directed his allegiance toward other abstractions and institutions. But I must have forgotten that his grandfather was a resistance fighter in Belgium in World War II. I must have forgotten that my own father was an anti-labor Taft Republican — or that Dad taught me to shoot a rifle at tin cans on a cactus when I was less than ten.

No, the issue of "where he came from" is teasingly complex, and fraught with hindsight. I have a black-and-white snapshot of Tim and his little brother, both of them tow-headed and long-lashed, squatting in an orchard full of daffodils. I also own a color photograph taken in the African savanna, of my grown elder son kneeling over the carcass of a wild boar, surrounded by his wiry, smiling Camaroonian guides. (One image I hold in my head, of the convolutions of honor, is of Tim, White Hunter, being mocked by these guides because, rigorous about the rules of the sport, he was unwilling to poach on government land. They thought he was afraid.) Now, looking at the toddler in the daffodils, I can see the clear lineaments of the hunter's face. But squatting beside him I had no premonition of which planes, tilts, colors of that cherub head would survive. Looking back, I can see clearly that his passion for little plastic planes, the tank kits he painstakingly put together with glue on the point of a toothpick, the bags of khaki-colored soldiers on whose webbing belts he layered a patina with a one-hair brush, the history books of famous battles, the catalogs of insignias of rank — in all that, I can see that his direction was early set. But I was a first-time parent. I thought all boys played soldier. Alex liked little planes too, and it did not absolutely register that by the time he was ten Alex had given up soldier stuff and gone into other fantasies, to Dungeons and Dragons and from thence to the Society for Creative Anachronism — veering from the mainstream, satirical toward patriotism, cocky about his pacifism: *Hey, man, okay, I'm afraid of you, I'd a whole lot rather talk it out, okay?* (In such wise, my younger son faced and survived some serious dangers of his subversive lifestyle. Nevertheless, there was a period when he was grateful for his big brother's prowess on the playground. Alex *would* wear a diaper pin in his ear, and Tim would beat up the bully that called him fag.)

I have witnessed, in my younger son, the astonishing but quite usual transformation from radical-punk-anarchist to responsible-loving-husband-breadwinner. The journey with Tim has been otherwise: it is I who have come to understand that this is who he is, and has been consistently from babyhood.

As a child Tim was modest, intense, fiercely honorable, and had few but deep friendships. He lit with enthusiasm for his most demanding teachers, praising their strictness, their discipline. Once he wailed at me for mentioning pajamas in front of dinner guests, and once when a new puppy crapped on the doormat he informed me that I kept an unsanitary house (I handed him the soap and rag). At this distance I can see that the Spock upbringing I struggled to offer, and which suited his little brother, was anachronistic to Tim's Victorian or even chivalric character. He has admitted as much, saying that though he was glad of the freedom I gave him, nevertheless his own children will have their boundaries drawn tighter.

Tim was from the beginning a worrier after his own integrity, which he pursued with solemn doggedness, eyes popping. Once when we were living near a woods in Tallahassee, the boys discovered a cache of professional archery equipment, hidden in its original manufacturer's carton in a hollow log in a ravine. The label bore an address to a local sporting goods shop. Alex and I stretched the long bows, admired the glossy laminated woods, and wavered, tempted. But Tim was clear and adamant: we had to drive to the shop to return it *right now*. It turned out that the equipment had been delivered to, and stolen from, a city park recreation center. I was somewhat sheepish in the face of my son's virtue, and annoyed that neither the shop nor the city so much as acknowledged his honesty, for which, however, Tim seemed to need no reward.

As he came to puberty he developed no interest in sports but had a keen eye on world news. He read voraciously, mostly adventure novels, admired John Wayne's acting and his politics, and more than once to my despair quoted, "My country right or wrong." At eighteen he came home at three one morning, in tears because he could not go to defend England's honor in the Falklands. About that time I realized that both my boys, who had spent their early years in shoulder-length blond shag, had shaved their heads — Alex for a Mohawk and Tim for ROTC. Both wore combat boots, the one for busking around the Eros statue in London, the other for jumping out of airplanes at Fort Benning. At that point I added to my theory of "where he came from" that Tim was rebelling against sixties parents, the ones who had him out in the stroller at the sit-ins or confined to his playpen while we addressed envelopes for Mothers Against the Bomb. Alex, instead of rebelling against Mom (what's the point? — if she'll let you be a soldier, she'll let you be anything), rebelled against his big brother, the hero worship and the Top-Siders, all things button-down or flag-waving.

Much of the time it seemed funny, and much of the time I had to acknowledge that when we fought, my battles with Alex were the more bitter precisely because he and I were more alike. His impulses were generous, sloppy, and full of turmoil, whereas Tim would hold back and calmly stand his ground. Alex was a loud and messy liberal, like me. Tim said "Yes, ma'am," ready to do a task right now, and I had to be grateful for military virtues in a son.

Nevertheless I knew that when I disagreed with Tim, there was a higher proportion of subtext to text. Our quarrels were less frequent and less personal, but they betrayed a deeper divide. In his late teens Tim went through a period in which he enjoyed goading my liberal friends with army swagger. He thought it was smart to interrupt them with tough talk. He had a bumper sticker that said, "This vehicle is protected by Smith & Wesson," and T-shirts with skulls and crossed rifles. Embarrassed, angry, and ashamed, I found no effective thing to say. I was grateful for the friend who told him, "You know, it isn't that we're shocked. All of us are familiar with the attitudes you have; we've considered and rejected them." Tim took this in. He swallowed and said, "I didn't think of it that way."

Since then he has thought of it in several hundred ways, and so have I. He spent four years in the army, the happiest time of his life, and later still ran security forces in the Camaroons, guarding the embassies and the multinationals. He loved the army, deplores cruelty, fights bigotry — but disciplined his African troops in a way that *they* called fatherly. He is a self-described capitalist, but the only job he ever despised was as a financial consultant ("Those sleaze-balls"). He is a swaggerer and an accomplished cook, a computer whiz with the soul of a musketeer. I'm forced to be aware of my own contradictions in his presence: a feminist often charmed by his machismo, a pacifist with a temper, an ironist moved by his rhetoric. Tim can still set my teeth on edge speaking in acronyms or the metaphors of battle, then disarm me with a self-put-down reference to "evolving guidance" (behavior of an officer who doesn't know what he's doing) or the SNORT in Sierra Leone ("Short Notice Over-Reaction Team"). His rhetoric can be Hemingwayesque, his humor heavy-handed; he can be quick to bristle and on occasion hidden far back in himself. On the other hand, these faults unfold his virtues: you would trust him with a secret on which your life depended; neither will he betray you in trivial ways. He would, literally, lay down his life for a cause or a friend. He is, of American types, pre-Vietnam.

Tim doesn't expect a weapon for his birthday, and I don't defend Jimmy Carter in his presence. But sometimes our ritual avoidances fail and we stumble into uneasy territory. I recall in particular an afternoon that I sat in my home office grappling with some inane, arcane university review, when Tim appeared in my doorway enthusiastically to opine, "The trouble with the university is that it ought to be run more like a business."

I blew up. "What the hell makes you think you know anything about running a university?" The stack of pointless paper on my desk was precisely the result of corporate-think in the administration. I flailed it in the air. "You and the idiot legislature."

He retreated coldly, withdrawing in more ways than one, and there were a couple of days of silence between us. Then I left a message on his machine, he left a reply on mine, we agreed to lunch on Monday and talked it through. I explained the nature of faculty governance, and pointed out that industrial studies showed autonomy in the workforce increased, not decreased, productivity. He argued that although tenure protected academic freedom, it also protected instances of sloth. I used the word "productivity," he said "academic freedom," which means that we found again the safe, familiar ground. But beyond this politesse we also came to acknowledge and agree that, mother and child, we not only don't share a worldview but *cannot respect each other's worldviews*. Our task is to love each other in the absence of that respect.

It's a tall order. We agreed that we do pretty well at it. The very stating of the impasse seemed paradoxically to confirm our respect. And Tim is broad-minded enough to add this observation: "It's a good thing it's you who's the liberal, mom. If I was the parent I wouldn't want to let you be you the way you've let me be me."

There are two things at work here: that motherhood is thicker than politics, and that a politics of certainty — the snap judgement, the closed mind, the blanket dismissal — cannot be what I mean by liberal. Tom Stoppard speaks in *Lord Malquist & Mr. Moon* of the "liberal cerebrum and conservative viscera." When I encountered that phrase I felt guiltily gratified, and in my most honest moments I acknowledge it again, because deeply to love where you deeply disagree creates a double vision that impinges daily in unexpected ways.

My grandfather was a small-town Republican banker. My parents were right-wingers of the working class, anti-smoking tee-totaling anti-union Methodists. My mother did TV spots for Goldwater in the fifties. When my first novel came out, my mother injudiciously showed me some letters she had received from friends, making it clear that she had written to them apologizing for the sex scenes I had written, curse words I had used. "Well, you know," I overheard her once say on the phone, "you have to put that in, or your books don't sell." My brother pointed out the ethical dilemmas my characters faced, their spiritual quests. "Mom, you keep defending her by saying she's sold out. Don't you understand what you've raised here is a Methodist moralist?"

But my parents were never able to see that though the forms in which I expressed myself were different and sometimes opposite from theirs, the underlying principles were the same. This half-blindness led to bitterness on their part and to lies on mine. I don't want to make the same mistake. Tim says: "Whatever you think of the warrior spirit, it isn't directed at self and it isn't devoted to money. It needs an extreme integrity." Rearrange the syntax a little, switch the nouns around, you might hear the rhythm of this sentence in my grandfather's mouth, my mother's, or my own.

The mail and the gun show were on Saturday. Sunday afternoon Tim is back to show me a double-cowhide holster he has cut, tooled, and stitched freehand. "It's a pretty fair copy of John Wayne's favorite; he called it his Río Bravo."

"It's handsome," I say. I don't say that it's also delicate, with bursts of flowerets burned around the curve of the holster front and the loop that holds it to the leg.

"I need to make some kind of finger protection." Tim shows me deep cuts in his index fingers from pulling the beeswaxed linen thread through hand-punched holes. "You have the awl in one hand and the needles in both, you mark the seam line and punch through, then thread one needle from the blind side and the second from the front."

I recall for him how I had to rent industrial machines to get through the leather when I costumed a play full of peasants in jerkins.

"The leather needle is shaped like a three-bladed triangle knife."

"So is the machine needle."

All those years while I taught my boys to iron and sew, I thought I was turning out little feminists. At Fort Benning Tim was laughing-proud to be the only one in his barracks who could put his military patches on his uniform with a sewing machine. He can cuff his own pants and press a perfect sleeve. It never occurred to me these skills would be put to use on cartridge belts and camouflage. But why not? How many swashbuckling-hero Halloween costumes did I sit and sew?

I must be confident of our accord today because it is I who ask him what he thinks of the situation in Iraq. I'm not sure what I think. Both of us have been following this week's particular crisis, he on CNN and I on NPR. Does he think Sadam Hussein should have been tracked down at the end of the Gulf War?

"Sure, but it wasn't that easy. He had good doubles, and kept moving. Our intelligence has always been heavy on the technology — radar, satellites, aerial photography. But we're a joke for intelligence personnel. The British would be better at it."

Over the course of an hour our conversation ranges from Hussein to "deniability" to the general question of truth between the military and the media, to free speech, to assumptions buried in the English language, to our apparent helplessness in Bosnia, to our sins of commission or omission in Africa, to the distinction between spirituality and belief. While he talks, in the course of a few sentences I can wince, be convinced, be aware that he knows much more than I do not just about matters military but also about history in general and current politics in the other hemisphere, let pass what I hear as a faulty syllogism or false logic, leap in to add a confirming point in some area of my own knowledge, or feel that on some issue or other I must protest. No doubt he goes through much the same range. Because today I'm thinking in this double way, listening to us as we talk, I'm also aware that the points on which I find him most convincing, or perhaps on which we most readily agree, are those suggesting that there is little remedy, or no clear choice among options.

On Bosnia he says, "We have to decide either to get out and let them sort it, knowing that means they go back to war and they'll kill each other till they're sick of it. Or else we have to commit to a whole generation — military presence, education, political intervention, and oversight. I don't know which is right. But I know we have to do one thing or the other. And if we do get out, we wasted the ones who died there."

He has another gun to show me, one I've seen in various stages of its perfecting. I forget the name of this one, a semi-automatic from which, he carefully shows me, he has removed the clip. He has spent several hundred hours filing every edge inside and out so that all the parts fit with silken smoothness and the barrel blackly shines. This is the hammer and the seer, the housing, the clip well. This is the site he's got an idea how to improve. This is the handle he has crosshatched with several hundred hair-width grooves to perfect the grip. Just so do I worry my lines across the page one at a time, take apart and refit the housing of the sentences, polish and shine. This is love of craft he's talking. This is a weapon that could kill a person I am holding in my hand. The conflict between conviction and maternal love stirs again, stressfully.

Bonnes Anniversaires

ate September and early October are dense with generation. Apparently it's a fact that more human nativity occurs in this period than at any other time of year. ("It's cold in January," my mother used to say, glancing aside. It was as risqué a remark as she ever addressed to me.) I'll be sixty on Saturday, and because the doctor says that this grandchild will surely not arrive before next Tuesday, Peter and I decide we'll take the Chunnel train to Paris for the weekend. We had hoped the baby might make me a birthday present of its birth, but in any case it's a lucky accident that we are teaching in London this fall, where we'll be nearby for the first two months of its life. Everywhere we look the streets are full of double pushchairs, newborns in babypacks slung against back or bosom, bellies showing their buttons against stretch Lycra.

The papers, too, are full of birth and birthdays, pointing out milestones at the outskirts of the microcosm. This week will mark Andrea Dworkin's fiftieth; Winnie Mandela will be sixty, and so will Flash Gordon. Brigitte Bardot is telling all and looking haggard at sixty-two. I share, apparently, a year of appearance with *Gone with the Wind* and a day with Larry Hagman. Janet Gaynor, for whom I was named Janet Gay, won the first Best Actress Oscar in the year of my birth. (She played a prostitute. Somebody pointed out to me that this year the actresses' Oscars were awarded to the roles of nun and whore; *plus ça change* . . .) The London *Independent* is entering its teens. *New Letters* is preparing its twenty-fifth anniversary issue and heading for the period of maximum fecundity. *Woman's Hour* is forty. The BBC *Third Programme* hits midlife crisis at fifty. Pinewood Studios, cradle of British film, is so vigorous at sixty that it hasn't time to stop and celebrate. F. Scott Fitzgerald would be a hundred on Tuesday if he hadn't died;

one news item tells me that this year will mark the fiftieth anniversary of the death of Gertrude Stein, though I'm not sure an entire year can be claimed for an anniversary. Never mind the millennium — everywhere decades are spotted out for significance, and I remember the New Math (which is now, I believe, the Superseded Math or the Abandoned Math, and reminds me cruelly of the passing of prime), noting that if we had eight fingers we would see ourselves significantly leaping forth at forty-eight and fifty-six.

The whole subject smacks of numerology and magic-making. I've never staggered over a birthday with a zero in it; rather vaunted my late-wrinkling DNA and my survival. But when I turn to the personal anniversaries, they loom with real meaning; their count thickens every year, and swells with those of an autumnal cast. This week I will be sixty and my first grandchild will be born. In the next few weeks will pass the anniversaries of my brother's birth and his wife's death, of my father's birth and of his death, my son's birth and his partner's birth and his father's death. One of the fulcrums of life must be when the annual turn of significant propagation comes round no more often than the dates of mourning. It's a year since buoyant Mark died, who was my age; and six months since Jerry, with whom I shared so many birthday parties over the years, died younger than I by three years.

This last loss weighs with a leaden irony, since my major memories of Jerry are of the voracious appetite of his mind, which brain cancer emptied in a matter of a few months. This week is full of early wakings; not exactly dark nights of the soul, merely sour and smudged. I see with surprise that I'm taking sixty hard. Or I'm pregnant with the eccentric of myself, with the curmudgeon. Old people are crusty because their tolerance for repetition declines; the crone temper flares *been-there-done-that*. It's also a physical reality that the days grow short as you reach September. It takes longer to wake and longer to climb the stairs. In the older house of the body the ratio of maintenance to construction shifts. Long before anybody out there sees you breathing hard or breaking stride, the memory skips, the joints suffer slippage, you discover old people don't walk that way because they're old, they walk that way because they *hurt*. When I see a superbly acted *Traviata* from a badly angled theater chair, the scene of Violetta's dying conveys not opulent melodrama but the knowledge that she's got a cramp in her lungs; she's woozy, and probably constipated.

It's no surprise that my predawn dismay is displaced into worry for the unborn newborn. What is surprising is that the worry is for life itself. Not that he or she will be scarred or fail to have ten toes. Not even that the world, its front pages splashed with Palestinian and Kabuli gore, is too cruel a place. Not drugs or disease or corruption or poverty, but that the acquisition of knowledge is so full of effort and so full of pain. Dutifully prepared to be awed by the miracle of a baby's learning, I stare aghast at the vast requirements of it: that multiplication and i-before-e, the square of the hypotenuse and Manifest Destiny and blank verse and existentialism and chaos theory must at such tedious cost be mote by mote acquired, most of it to be superseded, abandoned, discredited, and unlearned. And that's only schooling. The first heartbreak must also be learned, the first betrayal, the first vomitus drunk, the social grief, the self-deceptions. I am tired as if it were I and not this yet-gender-unknown other who must go through these hoops, these tiresome and triumphant passages, this thrilling waste. For someone so enamored of pattern as I am, so in love with the cyclical, the rhymed, the moment of closure, it is dislocating to feel such dread. Waking at five, on the edge of three score years, I find myself one of the Forster goblins of Beethoven's Fifth, not aggressive, merely walking the universe from end to end, observing that there is no such thing as splendor or heroism in the world.

Going to the Continent used to be a young man's game, the Channel perilous for a wooden craft in a rough sea, the Grand Tour about as dangerous as a Nepalese climb or an African elephant hunt. Now in three hours we are whisked out of London, under the water, and into Gare du Nord in time for dinner and a movie. We check into a little hotel on a side street off the Place de la Bastille.

The morning of my birthday Paris is crisp and clear. We nip into the coiffeur next door for smart Parisian haircuts. Then we round the corner into the Place, where seven or eight hundred people are congregated in a celebratory and slightly belligerent mood in front of a platform with a booming loudspeaker. Most of the crowd wear red caps or scarves, hold red helium balloons with the letters FO imprinted on them. A cumulus of a few thousand such balloons hangs over the podium ready for release, while a voice exhorts us in French too distorted by the speaker system for me to understand, though I can make out *fraternité* and *capacité* and *les droits universelles*. Someone shoves into my hand a brochure on which I am startled to see

60 ans!

The cover bears cartoon emblems marked 1936 and 1996. I am, I learn, the same age as French solidarity, the Force Ouvrier; my birth coincided with the winning of the forty-hour workweek and the principle of paid vacation. But I have forgotten what the word *chaumage* means, so I ask a man nearby, who explains with a face of urgent sympathy, "the people who have no work to do." Now I understand from the brochure that in France as in America and Britain, the official unemployment figures distort the plight of the out-of-work because they drop from their rolls all those who have ceased to search or hope. The man is wearing a red scarf and a tweed jacket, his fingertips on the elbow of his wife, who jiggles a pushchair with the other hand. In the chair sits a child of indeterminate gender, playing with the string of the balloon looped to its wrist. This child has a brushstroke of pale red hair and very intense dark eyes. The eyes do not look at the balloon, which is too far overhead to be of interest, but concentrate entirely on the string. The baby pulls the string very deliberately down to its bundled lap, then suddenly withdraws the hand and watches the string rise and straighten with a tug on the loop around its wrist. "Ooh," says the baby, and does it again. At something less than a year this child has sufficient experience of stringlike phenomena to calculate that this one is not behaving normally. "Oooh." This child is not among the unemployed. It is a member of the *force ouvrier*, working on the properties of helium.

"It's called labor," I enthuse to my daughter-in-law Tricia, who is mountainous and glowing, robust and cheerful, "for a reason." I know I am pontificating in the manner of grandmothers. "Other pains have to be endured or diagnosed, but this one is effort you put out expecting a return, so you deal with it a different way."

Monday and Tuesday pass. Wednesday comes and goes. Thursday night falls. The earth slides between sun and moon, and in a labor no longer than a Chunnel ride to Paris, there she is. It's a girl! Born in the darkest part of a night made blacker by eclipse: pink, perfect, hair dark and fingers long, ten of them, and ten toes. Seven pounds six ounces. Wailing and wanting. Age zero and counting.

Many happy returns of the day, Eleanor.

Acknowledgments . . . .

These essays are reprinted, sometimes in altered form, with permission from the following publications.

"I Didn't Know Sylvia Plath" from *Five Points*, Spring 2001.

"Danger and Domesticity in the Deep South" from *Sun Dog Review*, 4:2 (Fall 1982).

"Embalming Mom" from *Apalachee Quarterly*, 22 (1985).

"Footprints" (as "Empty Houses") and "Eleventh Hour" (as "Nothing Was Stirring") from *St. Petersburg Times*, October 31, 1984, and December 19, 1984.

"Changes" from *A Certain Age*, edited by Joanna Goldsworthy, Virago, 1993.

"We Eat the Earth" from *We Are What We Ate*, edited by Mark Winegardner, Harcourt Brace, 1998.

"Soldier Son" from *Between Mothers and Sons*, edited by Patricia Stevens, © 1999 by Patricia Stevens, reprinted with the permission of Scribner, a Division of Simon & Schuster, Inc.

"Dad Scattered" is reprinted with permission from *The Day My Father Died*, edited by Dianna Ajjan, © 1994 by Running Press Book Publishers, Philadelphia and London.

The following were first published in *New Letters* and are reprinted here with the permission of *New Letters* and the Curators of the University of Missouri-Kansas City: "Freeze Frame" 60:3 (July 1994); "Trash Talk" 60:4 (October 1994); "Pool" 61:4 (September 1995); "My One True West" 62:2 (April 1996); "PC and PC" 62:3 (June 1996); "*Bonnes Anniversaires*" 63:1 (January 1997); "Of the Beholder" 63:4 (December 1997); "Soldier Son" 64:2 (March 1998); "We Eat the Earth" 64:4 (November 1998).

My thanks to James McKinley and Robert Stewart of *New Letters*, at whose friendly urging many of these essays were written; to my editor Holly Carver at the University of Iowa Press, who makes the process a pleasure; and to John Mulvihill, my copyeditor, who has saved me from multiple minute humiliations.

Sightline Books . . . .
The Iowa Series in Literary Nonfiction

Embalming Mom: Essays in Life
JANET BURROWAY

No Such Country: Essays toward Home
ELMAR LUETH